THE VISION

By the same author:

The Vision

An antidote to post-charismatic depression

GERALD COATES

KINGSWAY PUBLICATIONS
EASTBOURNE

First published 1995
Reprinted 1995

Unless otherwise indicated, biblical quotations are from the New
International Version © 1973, 1978, 1984 by the
International Bible Society.

ISBN 0 85476 446 1

Produced by Bookprint Creative Services
P.O. Box 827, BN21 3YJ, England, for
KINGSWAY PUBLICATIONS LTD
Lottbridge Drove, Eastbourne, E. Sussex BN23 6NT.
Printed in Great Britain.

To the late Malcolm Muggeridge, whose writings and friendship meant more to me than he ever knew. Also to Ravi Zacharias whose writings and friendship made Jesus more attractive and intelligible. Can anything be more wonderful than that? Thank you.

Contents

Acknowledgements

It is of course impossible to thank all of those who have had an influence on me as a writer: through observation, dialogue and, quite often, through lifestyle, many have helped to shape my thoughts. While not directly involved in this book, they have been the cause of adjustments in my thinking and attitude over the years. I am grateful to each one, knowing that the Great Book Keeper has noted every 'cup of cold water' and every other act which has influenced others for good.

Particular credit must go to George Barna for his fine writings regarding vision; to William DeArteaga for his writings on the Holy Spirit and Scripture; to Roger Forster who gave me a theology on which I could hang my prophetic spirit; and to John Noble whose wisdom has at times got under my skin and annoyed me, but being under my skin has affected both my writings and my general ministry.

I also want to acknowledge the grace that Kingsway have shown me as I have endeavoured to write this book between growing responsibilities with our own church, Pioneer People in North East Surrey, our growing network of Pioneer churches, our work with March for Jesus, remaining an advisor to ACET and Pioneer Romania Aid, as well as my much reduced but nevertheless time-consuming travels. The manuscript was late in arriving, but I hope not the worse for that.

Thanks are also due to Derek Brown, who inspired me with the phrase 'post-charismatic depression'.

Last but by no means least my thanks to Amanda Collins my PA/Secretary who has typed the entire manuscript amid many other responsibilities.

An Explanation

The vision

A hope or dream, as yet unfulfilled. The focus that keeps
an individual or church on course. Primarily it must be
to see the world (or our personal world) evangelised for
Christ, with the understanding that this eschatological
activity will 'hasten his coming'. Individual visions will
supplement and complement the overall vision.

The mission

A journey with a purpose. The means through which the
vision is fulfilled. Local, national and international
initiatives need to learn from each other to fulfil the
vision. Many individuals and churches go round in
circles: God goes in a straight line.

The cost

The sacrifice of personal ambition and perspective to the
vision and the mission. For anything truly to flourish the
seed has to die. Many visions remain unfulfilled and
many missions unaccomplished because people are not

prepared to pay the price of seeing the vision become reality. What is the price? Radical discipleship.

The church

The main tool through which Christ's kingdom is revealed and communicated. The kingdom is larger than our vision or our understanding of it, but the people of God are the main channels (within relational networks and geographical localities) through which Christ and his benevolent rule are expressed and understood.

1

Embracing a Vision

*Was it a vision
or a waking dream?
Fled is that music:
Do I wake or sleep?*
Keats 'Ode to a Nightingale'

Why do we need an 'antidote to post-charismatic depression'? Isn't it true that thousands of charismatic Christians are enjoying great personal blessing these days? The so-called 'Toronto blessing' has erupted on to the scene, and Christians are being refreshed as God pours out his Spirit with sometimes embarrassing and even hilarious results. (More on this later in Chapter 7.)

You might think that any problems we may have had are now solved, but not so. Quite apart from the pastoral wisdom needed when meetings are constantly characterised by people falling on top of each other, or making too much noise for anyone to hear the sermon, the question remains: for all our sense of personal blessing, do we know what we are here for?

My greatest concern and fear is that these times of refreshing, which in many places have gone much deeper than refreshing, will come and go. Without a vision, and the strategy to fulfil the vision, there will be further 'post-charismatic depression'.

We need a biblical vision and a God-given strategy.

What is the church's vision statement?

A depressed world

Outside the church, the picture remains bleak. A few years ago, politicians were full of hope and vision for a post-Cold-War world. The promise of the 'New World Order' presented by President George Bush led us to believe that we stood on the threshold of a new age. The Berlin Wall had fallen, separated peoples were embracing, new trading markets were opening up. It was a new day in preparation for a new millennium.

However, it was not only the Berlin Wall which fell. So did expectations that things would be any different. The problems of racism, sexism and nationalism marking so many people groups, nations and religious communities—far from receding—grew in intensity. The dangers did not evaporate as expected; rather they simply changed location. The USSR ceased to be a threat, but now China has begun to emerge as the greatest long-term provocateur. Communism overall is dying of boredom internally while Muslim Fundamentalism is rising and has been embraced with violence and bloodshed. While some people were reconciled across old divides and borders, a quarter of a million people were slaughtered in Europe's former Yugoslavia, 20,000 mainly Muslim women were raped, often systematically and repeatedly (by way of retaliation) and all that was left of many exquisite towns was bombed-out shells.

So much for the new world order of peace and reconciliation between black and white, young and old, brown and yellow, male and female, rich and poor—or of standing and working together for an improved and hope-filled future.

As Malcolm Muggeridge wryly commented, 'The news is simply the same old things happening to different people.'

Nobody expected a perfect world, but a peaceful world, a loving world, a 'softer and kinder' world seemed, for a moment, within reach.

Who is running this thing?

I have limited experience in my own country concerning British Members of Parliament and Peers. One thing we can be sure of, however, is that neither the House of Commons nor the House of Lords is filled with evil men and women. Little men and women maybe, for it is of course impossible to produce great men and women of character, integrity and stature when money, fame and personal fulfilment are dangled as the purpose for an individual's existence. The world is full of little people who have chased those goals.

For example, Saddam Hussein may be viewed as a tyrant, but he is simply embodying what so many believe when they cannot get their own way—that might is right. Madonna may be dismissed for her brazen, sexual lyrics and performances, but she is only presenting publicly what so many foster privately: that if only all restrictions were removed from our culture we could have sex when we want, with whom we want (opposite or same sex) and hey presto, life would be fulfilling. So there we have it: megalomania or erotomania! Little people with little visions.

Most world leaders and influencers, the movers and

shakers, whether they be government leaders or entertainers, are often little people. They are not in the main evil people, but by spiritual standards they are basically as confused as those they are leading. They are at sea without a rudder. Many are lost in a moral maze. My experience with British politicians is that the majority are helpful but not hopeful. MPs are tireless workers and titled worriers. And they have plenty to worry about.

Early vision is now faded and blurred. The important is obliterated by the immediate. Few politicians, leaders within the business community, artists and entertainers have vision for anything other than themselves or people of their own kind. Thank God for the exceptions, but they are exceptions.

We live in a crazy world. Sectarian interests, whether in business or in gay rights, in religion or in Party politics, drown out the voice of vision, reason and reconciliation. Those same sectarian interests drown out the voice of God, and the voice of sanity, morality, health and hope. As G.K. Chesterton observed, 'When people cease to believe in God, they don't believe in nothing, they believe in anything!'

So supposedly sensible people in the latter years of the twentieth century actually believe a bunch of planets, floating around in the universe, affect their temperament, relationships and destiny! And all of this in a scientific age! As one leading astronomer quipped, 'There is more gravitational pull from the hands of the nurse when one is born, than all the solar systems put together!' Yet virtually all 'popular' newspapers carry the unscientific and irrational 'stars' forecast.

Others believe that sticking one's private parts into

every imaginable orifice will bring a life of fulfilment, happiness and satisfaction. This is despite the fact that far more people are dying of AIDS in America (85% contracted through homosexual and heterosexual promiscuity) than were killed in the entire twelve-year Vietnam War. Personal fulfilment and condoms galore leave us not with thousands, tens of thousands or even hundreds of thousands, but millions of people throughout the Western world who are now HIV-positive. The majority will eventually die of full-blown AIDS. A slow and frightening end.

Death and decay

Friedrich Nietzsche, arguably the most influential thinker to have affected this century, came to the conclusion that 'God is dead'. Laying aside the questionable causes of how he came to that conclusion, he wrote savage articles against Christian people in the press and gave similar speeches. He then made a startling prediction. He explained that if, from a philosophical point of view, God was now dead, and there was no room for him in the monarchy, business, government, art, industry, education, medicine, family life or individual morality, two things would happen. First, this century would be the bloodiest of all time. Secondly, universal madness would break out.

One does not have to be an historian to see that those two predictions have not only been fulfilled in this century, but increasingly in our own lifetime.

The British songwriter Noel Richards and I sought to reflect this in a recently written hymn.

Great is the darkness that covers the earth, oppression injustice and pain;

Nations are slipping in hopeless despair,
Though many have come in your name.
Watching while sanity dies,
Touched by the madness and lies.

Come Lord Jesus, come Lord Jesus,
Pour out your Spirit we pray.
Come Lord Jesus, come Lord Jesus,
Pour out your Spirit on us today.

The darkness and madness are everywhere, it seems. The United Nations endeavouring to feed the hungry ends up killing the innocent and feeding the perceived enemy. The United Nations has become a toothless wonder—merely a mobile hospital for corporate terminal illness. Global bullying continues, initiated by despots and gutless wonders. Despite the longings and groanings of a watching, mesmerised audience, there is unlikely to be, as Charles Krauthammer wrote, an 'immaculate intervention'.

The world, it seems, is hallucinating on an overdose of fantasy and delusion. Raised voices and fists leave little room for hope. So what do we have? Civilisation, rock 'n' roll style, with Madonna; or a new world order, military style, with Saddam Hussein.

Good intentions and worthy initiatives are not enough. Intellectually bankrupt and morally compromised, the God-given framework for sensible living has not been eroded, it has been blown to smithereens.

What the world needs, I suggest, is a vision from the One who made us. It follows that behind creativity there must be a Creator; behind personality a Person; behind beauty a beautiful energy; and behind love such a great divine source of care and compassion. The argument for a designer initiating design is compelling.

Of course the atheist would tell us there is no such Creator, no such source of beauty or love. I appreciate there are many difficult concepts that the Christian has to work through, especially those who read Scripture in order to understand our existence on this planet. The idea that God created something out of nothing is a difficult concept to get your mind around. But what is the atheist's alternative? That *nothing* created something out of nothing!

That, to me, and I suggest to most sensible people, is an even more difficult concept to get your mind around. I think I would rather embrace something that is infinitely more rational—indeed a notion that the sublimest souls have embraced—that there is a God, he does care, but our own wrongdoing, vested interest and sectarian pursuits drown out his vision and voice of reason.

God's world

Could it be that there was an original vision for this globe and its peoples? The Bible teaches that there was. The sixty-six books that make up Scripture, which we call the Bible, is not a book of doctrine (though it contains some of the most sublime teaching). It is an accurate record of God at work in human lives, families and people groups. This began with Adam of course, made in God's shape and texture. It continued with Noah's family, when wrongdoing and evil so saddened God he destroyed the very thing he had created, saving one family. (When you are God, you can do things like that!) So he moved from a man named Adam, to a family—Noah's. But he then moved onto Abraham, explaining that his seed, his offspring, would be as the 'sands of the earth'. This speaks of the earthly, biological people of Israel, the Jews. Despite successive regimes and tyrants endeavouring to restrict and at times annihilate the Jewish community, God has performed and stood by his word. Today we have American Jews, Polish Jews, English Jews, Russian Jews. They are indeed the 'sands of the earth'. Without number, it seems.

Later, God broadened his promise to Isaac, to another people group altogether. He went on to explain that his offspring would also be 'as the stars of heaven'. This is not now an earthly, biological people, but a heavenly people. Abraham put his faith in God when he was too old to have children, because of the promise. So through faith we have become the children of Abraham. Today there are far more non-Jewish believers than Jewish believers. Most Christians are not of the privileged, earthly stock of Israel as was Christ. We were without hope and without God. We were Gentiles, that is non-Jews. But this God has now become the God of Jew and Gentile, black, white, yellow and brown. So peoples of all colours, races, levels of education and social standing can pray together as Jesus taught: 'Your kingdom come, your will be done, on earth—as it is in heaven.'

God began with Adam, then blessed Noah's family. He enlarged his purpose to Abraham's biological offspring, then to Isaac and then to those who would live like Abraham, by faith—Jew and Gentile.

This is a heavenly kingdom where there is no racism, sexism or nationalism. Its fulfilment in the age to come is not saturated with sex, shrivelling cynics or well-intentioned but misbehaving agnostics or atheists.

Visionaries in the Old Testament

Almost every major biblical figure who served God had a vision.

Moses not only received instructions (the Law), but also a vision. He was the son-in-law of the Priest of Midian, pasturing Jethro's flock. He saw an angel in a burning bush and was intrigued as to why the bush was not consumed in the fire. He responded to this remarkable phenomenon saying, 'I must turn aside now and see this great sight, why the bush is not burned up.' It was when he 'turned' (which is symbolic of another kind of change of direction, repentance) that God spoke to him. It was during this encounter that he was given a clear vision and instructions as to how to fulfil that vision. That call, to co-operate with God 'to deliver the Israelites from the power of the Egyptians, and to bring them up from that land to a good and spacious land', filled his heart and mind for another forty years. In times of darkness, depression, squabbling and defeat, it was that call and vision that kept him on course.

Later, Joshua was to receive a call linked to a vision, although he was not a pioneer in quite the same way as Moses was. Moses, having been warned of his own death, prayed, 'May the Lord, the God of the spirits of all mankind, appoint a man over this community to go out and come in before them, one who will lead them out and bring them in, so that the Lord's people will not be like sheep without a shepherd.' God replied, 'Take Joshua son of Nun, a man in whom is the Spirit, and lay your hand on him. Make him stand before Eleazar the priest and the entire assembly and commission him in their presence. Give him some of your authority [majesty] so that the whole Israelite community will obey him' (Num 27:15–20).

A most interesting comment was made about Moses at his burial: 'Moses was a hundred and twenty years old when he died, yet his eyes were not weak nor his strength gone' (Deut 34:7). The physical no doubt reflected the spiritual—he was a man of vision. Joshua embraced that vision and took the people towards the Promised Land.

Visionaries in the New Testament

Turning to the New Testament, the Apostle Paul, who wrote more of it than any other writer, is seen as a man of obvious vision.

He was a man with options. People's options often hinder vision—they become paralysed by indecision. Despite these options Paul was single-minded. Born a Jew and schooled by the Greeks, he was also a Roman citizen. At one stage he must have been married (he was a member of the Sanhedrin, whose qualifications demanded you were married). He must have been well connected to get letters from the senior priests to persecute the followers of Christ.

Ravi Zacharias, the brilliant apologist, has pointed out that the Jews gave light to the world, the Greeks knowledge and the Romans the notion of glory. God knew what he was doing when he chose Paul, who was to the Jews a Jew, to the Greeks a Greek and to the Romans a Roman. Paul was of course to take the gospel way beyond the confines of the Jewish community. I often wonder whether Paul knew what he was writing when he penned, 'For God, who said, "Let light shine out of darkness," made his light shine in our hearts to give us the *light* of the *knowledge* of the *glory* of God in the face of Christ' (2 Cor 4:6, italics mine). There we have it: light, knowledge and glory 'in the face of Christ'.

Yet wherever Paul went, he worked hard, suffered imprisonment, was beaten 'times without number', received thirty-nine lashes from the Jews, was beaten with rods, stoned and on three separate occasions was shipwrecked and spent 'a night and a day' in the sea. He suffered dangers from robbers and pseudo Christians; he suffered sleepless nights, was hungry and thirsty, and he suffered the extremities of cold and exposure. Why? Because he was a man of vision.

The Apostle Paul was driven by vision and values. And he took both to the Jewish community and to the Gentiles, who until this time were without hope and without God.

Peter had already been challenged to take the gospel to the Gentiles. Having received a heavenly vision and having heard a heavenly voice, he was then taken to a centurion from the Italian battalion by the name of Cornelius. The reluctant evangelist explained about the life and ministry of Christ, his death on the cross and his resurrection. As Peter spoke, the Holy Spirit 'came on all who heard the message' (Acts 10:44), they spoke in tongues and Peter was unable to refuse them baptism in water. Peter then had to go back to Jerusalem, the church's HQ, to explain the unbelievable—that those outside of the covenant-keeping community of Israel were worshipping God, singing his praises and embracing the God of the Jews!

It has been said that Peter never really understood that his call was to take the gospel to the Gentiles, while Paul was to take it to the Jews. But Peter failed to perceive the phenomenal implications and ramifications of the gospel.

So Paul and his friend Barnabas at Pisidian Antioch, facing hostile Jews explained, 'We had to speak the word of God to you first. Since you reject it and do not consider yourselves worthy of eternal life, we now turn to the Gentiles. For this is what the Lord has commanded us: "I have made you a light for the Gentiles, that you may bring salvation to the ends of the earth"' (Acts 13:46–47).

Because of Paul's prolific, personal correspondence, we know that he went on at least five separate apostolic missionary journeys, evangelising tens of thousands of people, planting churches in teams of up to twenty-seven people and even addressing the highest people of the land. He evangelised the whole Aegean area— Greece. Then he set his sights on Spain, and although biblical material about this stage of his ministry is scarce, it is possible he covered most of the northern half of the Roman empire in his remaining years. In the last two of those recorded years, in his own rented quarters, he was 'preaching the kingdom of God, and teaching concerning the Lord Jesus Christ with all openness, unhindered'. We hear no more of him, although tradition tells us he was eventually put on trial and beheaded.

Christ our visionary Pioneer

Primarily, it is Jesus Christ himself whose vision for a new age, a new world order, fills the pages of the New Testament.

That vision started in an individual Man, touching families and local networks of the inquisitive and believing Jews. The growing company that followed Jesus—first the twelve, then the seventy, then the 500—would become tens of thousands of people. They were soon to be called 'the ekklesia', of which I write more later. This heavenly vision, and the means through which men and women could enter into that vision, reached royal palaces and business leaders, as well as commoners, the poor, the disenfranchised and the powerless.

This vision would unite races, and make inroads into the sexism that prevailed in those days. This vision was of a new humanity, where people would not treat each other on the basis of their gender or pigmentation of skin. It was a vision where both individuals and communities no longer judged one another on the basis of the clothes they wore, the homes they lived in, their means of transport or their financial standing.

It was six miles south of Jerusalem, in Bethlehem, where it all started. A life came into the world, took on human nature but not adult personality. The parents gave the baby the name Jesus, the Greek form of Joshua or Yeshua. He would also be known as the Christ, Greek for Christos, simply meaning 'anointed'.

Scientists have for centuries believed that the world is a closed universe, a continuum of cause and effect. But God has not abandoned the world to cause and effect, but was proactive in offering a remedy to the selfishness of individuals and the defensive and often offensive hostilities of entire nations. He was not only to bring forgiveness of sin, but he was to implant a new spirit, a visionary spirit, the Holy Spirit, to every repentant wrongdoer.

Jesus Christ devoted his life to embracing and fulfilling God's will for his life.

Recently I saw the musical *Buddy* at a London theatre. I was taken by surprise when we found that his professional recording career spanned a mere eighteen months. Yet how profound those eighteen months were. As I left the theatre it seemed everybody was humming 'Every day seems a little closer' or 'It really doesn't matter any more'. As I walked down the road, 'That'll be the day' and 'Peggy Sue' could still be heard as others sang 'Raining in my heart'. All that in eighteen months.

Yet it is likely that the Lord Jesus Christ had only a little more than eighteen months longer, not to get a generation singing a few songs, but to change the history of hundreds of millions of individuals, communities and, as it turned out, the entire culture of the Western world. In the light of the remarkable events in Africa and China, as well as parts of Asia where literally hundreds of thousands of people are turning to Christ each week, it is arguable that the entire world will have been touched by 'One Solitary life' by the end of this millennium.

As individuals, families and communities submit their vision to the eternal Creator, Saviour and Visionary, the world becomes a better place.

Vision, hope and suffering

Vision enthrals; it draws people up and out to higher things and can give immeasurable hope.

But to see a vision fulfilled demands careful thought, recognition of the skills and abilities of others, hard work, sacrifice and suffering. For the vision to be fulfilled—for a new humanity to work in the earth—Jesus suffered a despicable death on a Roman cross—considered to be one of the most cruel tortures ever devised. And from the lips of a man whose body had been beaten, his beard pulled out, three-inch thorns pressed into his head and having been nailed alive, spoke words that ring down the centuries: 'Father forgive them, they do not know what they are doing.'

The vision that Jesus read about in the Scriptures as a boy, teenager and young man (periods of life hidden from our view) prepared him for his mission. At the age of thirty he was baptised. As he stood there facing his cousin John the Baptist, the mission was about to begin.

Vision and mission are not the same thing. A vision is that which as yet is unrealised. A mission is a journey with a purpose. Jesus' journey with a purpose was about to begin. To forgive wrongdoers, to heal the sick, to deliver the oppressed and to share resources with the poor. Far from being acknowledged as the Creator and Saviour of the cosmos he was set up by Jewish leaders, was beaten and tortured by Roman soldiers and was eventually nailed to his own creation, a tree from a forest nearby. Yet none of this was for himself. Neither was it a mistake or accident. This was a deliberate choice, to bring salvation, forgiveness and wholeness to all the nations of the universe.

In a world occupied with personal survival or personal fulfilment, the Man, the universal Christ, stands before us, winning us and wooing us away from self-centredness, personal ambition and gain. He offers a vision to every born-again believer as well as the not-yet believer. It is an offer, not only of forgiveness and the gift of eternal life and the assurance of salvation in the age to come, it is the invitation to co-operate in bringing heaven to the earth. He taught us to pray, 'Your kingdom come, your will be done, on earth as it is in heaven.' For each of us, that means our part of the earth, and the people within that part of the earth in which we live, travel, function and conduct our leisure activities.

A focus for charismatic enthusiasm? Or an antidote for post-Cold-War depression? So much of the depression that was in the churches before 1994 (and still remains in many!) came out of a selfish desire to have our life, our ministry, our church, go the way we want it to. But when we step back, understand the vision of this Man, this Christ, and ask forgiveness for our self-centredness, laying aside our own agendas, we are kissed with his presence. Then we can be filled with a new vision for others, not ourselves; to serve and not to rule; to give away rather than gain and get.

New vision for New Churches?

We should not underestimate the impact of the crazy, corrupt and Christ-rejecting culture that surrounds us. Economic pressures often mean bills don't get paid on time. Negative equity can create the feeling of being trapped in a property for ever. As we grow older, sickness comes our way as well as the loss of parents and older Christian leaders. Most hurtful and depressing are those who were once our friends who now no longer walk with God or have withdrawn from friendship and fellowship with us. The pain that comes through economic pressures, sickness, disappointment and depression causes us to ask questions. What do we have to look forward to? Will our future be a rerun of our past? What if all our children grow up deciding not to follow the Lord? Do we really believe in heaven and hell?

In such situations, sin (albeit private religious

self-centredness) can become quite attractive. It beckons us on to deny that we are anything else other than human. Entire churches can become pleasant but virtually useless in making Christ attractive and intelligible to those who do not know him. Even intense spiritual experiences will not of themselves deliver answers for many people. What is crucial is obedience to our Master's vision statement.

Many churches, and particularly non-charismatic churches, do not have high expectations. Emotionally and psychologically individuals and churches are seen to receive teaching, worship with ancient hymns and pray in a quiet but orderly fashion. There is little or no expectation of immediate answered prayers, healing or outward manifestations of being filled with the Spirit. Spiritual gifts are never expected and rarely experienced.

By contrast, charismatics have expectations. Yet many are quite unrealistic. To hear some you would think they are talking about a Christianised government or education system; indeed an entire culture. As a result of more prayer here, spiritual warfare there, as well as getting out and about with the gospel, just about everybody is going to be converted and there will be little or no opposition. This is hardly the picture the Bible presents.

The way forward

Self-disillusionment *can* nevertheless be a pathway to maturity. Coming to terms with our limitations and powerlessness can turn us to Christ and to more power from his Holy Spirit. God only knows how much we need more power in our living, serving, preaching and teaching, as well as in prayer. Both in Scripture and contemporary history it is clear that some have more power than others.

But the greatest hindrance to moving forward to fulfil the vision, is the past.

I thank God for the outpouring of the Spirit which has renewed thousands of churches, stemmed the massive haemorrhaging and created New Churches. In Britain alone there are around one-and-a-quarter million evangelical believers, and a fifth of those are in the New Churches, both those who are networked to apostolic teams and others who are independent. Twenty-five years ago the number of New Churches (House Churches) were but a handful.

Friendships, relationships, community, praise and worship, and faith for something significant to happen have taken both individuals and churches forward. Disappointments, due to mistakes and unfulfilled expectations of growth and holiness, have in many cases slowed things down. In some cases they have almost slowed to a stand still. Change becomes difficult to implement.

Despite being in what some would regard as a large church, increasingly I have been asking God to help me see people the way he sees them. The unchurched are lost. There are almost 100,000 people living in the area in which we are working, and fewer than 1,000 of those are in Pioneer People, our church in North East Surrey just beyond South West London. Now in consultation with others we have decided that we would cancel one Sunday evening a month to invite neighbours in for meals, build bridges with the community and put on fun events, as well as visit institutions with friendship and the gospel. It would have to be said that a large percentage of the church responded to this initiative. Most people are very busy with work and many commute. There are probably at least two or three meetings a week for worship and teaching, prayer and some specialist group that most are involved in. So an evening off a month to reach out to the community seems sensible. But there was a significant minority who found not meeting once a week difficult. These were not the young people, but older people. We even lost some people over it. Given the fact that we have Christian books, cassettes, videos and fellowship, I sometimes imagine that if people who have been Christians for twenty years or more didn't go to a meeting of any sort for three months it would barely make any difference to their spirituality or effectiveness. In fact it could make them more effective as they reflect on how uncaring they have been to those we say are lost, and how wrapped up they have been in themselves. Pioneer People, the church I lead, is regarded to be one of the most go ahead if not radical churches around. But we cannot co-exist with the dichotomy of saying we believe in hell without reaching out to those who are lost. We cannot live with a healthy vision but unfulfilled purpose. We cannot talk about being flexible and radical when we resist most forms of change.

But there is a way forward. There is a way out of unfulfilled expectations, genuine disappointments, mid-life crisis and mid-church crisis.

So how do we get from here to there? From vision to reality; from aspiration to achievement? That's our mission!

2

Fulfilling the Mission

One of the pleasantest things in the world is going on a journey;
but I like to go by myself.
William Hazlitt, 'On Going on a Journey'

'Going it alone' is the mission of many and is not confined to William Hazlitt. But I suggest that going it alone, far from alleviating our ills, positively contributes to them. It is a course without reference to others, and contributes to the breakdown of communication, understanding and harmony in all sectors of society.

Vision is vital. Vision gives us something to live for; it focuses our attention in good times and bad. But how is vision fulfilled?

David Livingstone had a vision to take his Christian faith to Africa. To accomplish this he went on a mission. As we noted in the previous chapter, a mission is 'a journey with a purpose'.

What is the church's 'journey with a purpose'? It is to take God's love and indeed Christ himself, making both attractive and intelligible, to all people groups, especially the powerless and the voiceless.

Such a journey means forgiveness for wrongdoers, healing for the sick, deliverance for the oppressed and possessed, and the sharing of resources with the poor. It means patience for those in tribulation, hope for those lost in a sea of darkness, and friendship for those baptised in loneliness. This is good news—it is the gospel. This is God's message to the earth.

Jesus Christ exemplified this message perfectly. He was on a journey with a purpose, and he still is today.

The writer to the Hebrew Christians tells us that when Jesus came into the earth he made himself available. He had a vision, but he was now on a mission. Quoting from Psalm 40 he says, 'Sacrifice and offering you did not desire but a body you prepared for me . . . "Here I am—it is written about me in the scroll—I have come to do your will, O God"' (Heb 10:5, 7).

His quote from Psalm 40 is virtually perfect, but instead of the original reference to a 'pierced ear' he makes reference to his 'body'. At certain times of the Jewish calendar, particularly in the year of Jubilee, certain slaves would be set free. But slavery was not the sort of slavery we saw in America in the 1950s. Many slaves or servants were senior people with staff and budgets. The last thing they wanted was to be virtually thrown out of their home, job and responsibilities. So they became 'free slaves'. As a sign that they had quite freely chosen to stay with their master they had their ear pierced. It obviously spoke of the way the slaves were being looked after and reflected on the calibre of their master, but it was a life-long commitment.

So why change the phraseology of Psalm 40 with a new inclusion—that of the concept of a body? Well I suppose that if you have someone's ear you have their body!

I have a colleague who frequently visits my office, as he is part of a planning group for one of the Pioneer Ministries. It is not unusual for him to say, 'Can I have a

word in your ear?' at a suitable break or at the close of
our meeting. As my ear doesn't have a life of its own I
have to get up from behind my desk and move over to
another part of the office where he speaks to me
confidentially. If you have got someone's ear you have
got their body.

But in quoting from the Psalms our Lord says three
important things:

1. He finds his identity in Scripture (the scroll).
2. His mission is to do the will of God not merely the
   will of the government, the military, peer pressure or
   parental will.
3. This would get done through his body.

Paul's favourite type, metaphor and illustration for the
people of God is 'the body of Christ'. Perhaps this is
because he knew that it was through bodies—individual
and corporate—that God's will would primarily be
done.

Jesus and his mission

Looking at Jesus Christ as our model, we see he fulfilled
his mission with 'words, works and wonders'. All were
achieved through his body.

While it is true that certain scriptures are ambiguous
about 'greater works than these' and there have even
been questions about the validity of the closing verses of
Mark 16, the New Testament is awash with 'words, works
and wonders'. We do not have to base our theology for
such a gospel around a couple of scriptures.

Christ was the great communicator. Indeed, the only
things we know about the Godhead are those things
they have chosen to communicate to us human beings.

We know nothing apart from that. Creation itself speaks to us, as do the prophets, priests and kings. But primarily he has spoken to us through Jesus Christ. He is God's final word to a lost world.

However, communication takes place at several levels. My wife Anona doesn't need to use words when she gives me an embrace or cooks my favourite meal. Those actions communicate her love, care and tenderness in ways words cannot. But should there be a fire in our house, then a kiss, or bacon, egg and sausages, or a bar of bitter dark chocolate is highly inappropriate! In that situation we would need urgent and passionate words.

So if we are to fulfil our mission, we must communicate at different levels, just as Christ did.

Strategic mission

If a people group or a nation is to be effectively evangelised, it has been reckoned there needs to be a body of Christians for every 1,000 or so people. For the Christian faith to be seen, heard and experienced, it needs to be performed and outworked in a group of practising disciples in every geographic area among all cultures within that area.

Pioneer People in Surrey now covers several towns. Within those towns there is an upper-class population, complete with security gates, suspicion of visitors and ex-directory phone numbers. But we also have council estates with inadequate means of transport (both personal and public) and rising unemployment.

People groups relate at two levels. The first is geographic. The relationship between the Fairmile Estate in Cobham and the council estate is non-existent! Both have been caricatured and this hinders understanding. The second is cultural. The youth culture has little or nothing to do with the growing number of elderly people in private homes, council homes and institutions. To communicate effectively in our mission, we must live among and reach all people groups in those geographic and cultural areas.

But the church must demonstrate something other than homogenous groupings. Youth reaching youth is the starting point. But if they cannot be integrated into a wider church it only fosters divisions between the youth generation and the rest. Equally, the South African, American or black communities may well be ideal to reach those self-same people groups who as yet are without hope and without God. But once they come to faith, if we are unable to see them relate to a pigmentation of skin different from their own, we are simply furthering separate groups whose continual existence generates misunderstanding, caricature and quiet hostility.

The way forward

So, how do we move from our current agendas, structures and activities towards something that will reach the area in which God has placed us? How does one fulfil a mission?

1. Attitude

David faced this issue with Goliath. His response could have been either, 'What a size that man is! I don't stand a chance,' or, 'Boy, he is so big I can't miss him!' A humble but positive attitude is vital if we are to fulfil our mission.

2. Sensitivity

Reaching out to others demands proactive creativity. But being creative for the sake of creativity (which fails to communicate) comes across as weird. In-house language, Christian clubbiness, mitigates against effective communication. Clarity with respectful sensitivity is vital on this mission.

3. Structures

It is important to ask: 'Are our forms helping us or hurting us?' Structures cannot create growth, but they can impair growth. All local structures should be looked at with a radical eye. Jesus promised that if we were fruitful he would prune us, and if we were unproductive he would cut us down! This is the only way to effective, purposeful growth.

4. Team

Whenever God wants something done, he never appoints a committee! He always looks for a woman or man upon whom his Spirit rests, who has the courage and skills to fulfil the mission. Yet the church is not the arena for the lone ranger. Moses needed a team. The Apostle Paul needed a team. Even Jesus himself appointed a team immediately after his commissioning for the mission. Team gives the necessary checks and balances as well as the encouragement and safety net we all need.

5. Scripture

One does not need to be quoting the Bible in all communication in order to be biblical. It is assumed that the majority of those reading this publication

would call themselves evangelical or have a high view
of Scripture and its importance. Our difficulty therefore
in these latter years of the twentieth century does not
centre around the authority of Scripture, but how to
translate that authority into our culture. When the
Apostle Paul addressed those on Mars Hill in Athens,
he failed to quote the Old Testament and instead used a
well-known Cretan poem written for Zeus! ('For in him
we live and move and have our being.')

6. Stability

If we want people to be committed it is important that
they know what to expect. Shifting values, changing
visions and rotating personnel do not provide familiar
landmarks. Multi-generational congregations cannot be
expected to cope with extremes in an unannounced fashion. Blended styles may work, but in an unpredictable
age we need predictable landmarks.

7. Realism

Set goals, by all means, but be realistic. Depression sets
in when unrealistic goals of numerical growth and
effective outreach remain unfulfilled. Also, if an idea is
too complex, many will not even bother to try to achieve
it. Be realistic in expectations and goals, while adding
the dimension of faith. What many would call faith, I
would call absurd!

8. Reality

As a Christian, or church, don't get separated from your
real self, your genuine identity. Much of our ministry
demands a measure of performance, but performers can
become unhinged from reality. Give attention to

integrity so that spiritual schizophrenia does not take over. Only God can manage being a trinity!

9. Patience

Sowing seeds is not difficult, but creating an environment for them to grow in is more difficult. Patience is needed for the plant to flourish. I suggest it can be anything between six months and two years from the time the seed is sown in a group to the time people understand it to the degree they no longer have to talk about it. Be patient in whatever group you are working with. Ideas take time to become realities.

10. Support

Even in conflict, endeavour to be supportive. We cannot build relationships on the basis of what we do not appreciate about people, even though at times we have to express reservation and concern. Leadership that is not supported cannot be creative and cannot make mistakes. Be as supportive as you can, while allowing that leadership of the church (or a ministry within the church) has limitations and inadequacies.

The journey begins

Once we have declared our mission, that we aim to reach every household and people group with the gospel in our locality, the seed is sown. Further seed then needs to be sown in various groups within the church, from the house group to the youth group, from the business forum to prayer meetings. A little here, a little there, all done without pressure or condemnation, but with continual challenge. However, the church cannot live on continual challenge!

As a body of people journey, leadership changes will become necessary. What has got us to where we are may not get us to where we want to be. All sorts of forums and structures may need to be pruned or cut down. This is not a time for sentimentality. For the vision to be fulfilled, the journey with a purpose has to begin.

But there comes a time when movement creates momentum and momentum demands clear, sustained vision.

Sheriff Clark once confronted Dr Martin Luther King who was leading a peace march of thousands of citizens both black and white. 'Go back,' Sheriff Clark demanded. 'You will have to go back.' Dr Martin Luther King replied, 'We can't go back—we have come too far already.'

Once the journey has begun and there is momentum, there will come a time when you cannot go back. You can only go forward.

Somebody once said, 'Every area of change brings about a crisis of self-esteem.' It is true. Those who have done well under the old regime may feel they will not do so well under the new. So on the one hand there is the need for clarity; on the other humility, open-endedness and willingness to change instead of just expecting to see change in others.

While we put our faith in God, we have to face the fact that we may experience failure. In the introduction to my autobiography *An Intelligent Fire* I wrote, 'Success is the ability to survive failure.' Those who have never known failure are unlikely to succeed in the kingdom of God. Success without failure breeds arrogance, self-sufficiency and an inability to listen to others. The possibility of failure, while foreign to many of those who have been brought up to believe we should have faith in

God, takes a lot of pressure out of things. It also acknowledges our frail ability to understand the heart and mind of God as revealed in Scripture and through prophetic ministry today.

Look at Abraham Lincoln's journey with a purpose:

In 1831 he failed in business.
In 1832 he was defeated for legislature.
In 1833 he failed in business again.
In 1834 he was elected to legislature.
In 1835 his sweetheart died.
In 1836 he suffered a nervous breakdown.
In 1838 he was defeated for Speaker.
In 1840 he was defeated for Elector.
In 1843 he was defeated for Congress.
In 1846 he was elected to Congress.
In 1848 he was defeated for Congress.
In 1855 he was defeated for Senate.
In 1856 he was defeated for Vice President.
In 1858 he was defeated for Senate.

But in 1860 he became President of the United States of America!

We cannot undo some failures and we cannot right many wrongs from our past, but embracing a vision will lead us to a mission where failure will be experienced and mistakes made. It is then we have to understand that what happens *in* our lives is more important than what happens *to* our lives.

Hindrances

So what hinders a local church from a mission? What kills a vision stone dead?

Embracing a vision gives us cause to plan a mission—to fulfil the vision. In the next chapter we deal with the cost involved of fulfilling a mission. But before we get to the cost there is another issue—the issue of hindrances. Vision for a leader, the leadership team and a local church may well be clear: to reach every person, every household and every people group in our location with the gospel. This is a wonderful biblical vision, and this vision can translate into church planting in other localities doing a short-term mission project in another part of the nation or indeed overseas.

But hindrances can kill a vision stone dead. Strategy for mission can be bogged down before it moves off in the right direction. So how do we deal with those hindrances?

I have found in our own church seven issues that can be major hindrances.

1. We have never done it this way before

All churches start with a vision and some sort of mission, however limited. Any healthy church is made up of conservatives and radicals. Wise, mature Christians will know that what God is looking for is conservative radicals and radical conservatives—clever enough to know what qualities and values we must conserve and virile enough to know that we have to go to the root of our problems when it comes to reaching the lost. (Radical means we go to the root.) To be radical and go to the root means we must change. Change is threatening.

Our mission to fulfil the vision will be shaped up by the people groups we are endeavouring to reach, which means we are going to have to experiment and do new things. We must give time for the new to develop.

2. We are not ready yet

Our church has always had a healthy concern for the lost, but we have not always translated that into anything beyond prayer and friendship. Sure, there has always been a trickle of people coming to Christ, but it has been too little over too long a period of time to satisfy most of us. So we began to emphasise the gospel Sunday after Sunday, month after month in our regular celebration/teaching meeting. Our small cell groups are not only there for pastoral care and prayer, but also to reach out to not-yet Christians. Believe it or not, in a church that is regarded as being healthy, successful and radical, with a number of key national and international ministries attached to it, we found a major hindrance. Where did it come from? Surprisingly, it came from mature believers who had regularly prayed, tithed and given themselves in pastoral care to the Christian community. Many were involved in the Parent Teacher Association, or were governors of the local school; they helped out with Meals on Wheels and youth work for the County Council. But when the gospel came onto every personal agenda it was believers who had endeavoured to follow Christ for ten or twenty years who responded, 'We are not ready for that yet!' I confess I thought to myself, 'If we are not ready now to share our faith, we never will be.'

3. We seem to be OK without this

Most Christians need two forums. First, a small group (our church calls them Network Groups) where there can be care, intimate sharing and a care for the lost. The other is the large celebration/teaching event to help people feel a part of something larger than their own small group. The difficulty is, if you have a fairly trouble-free cell group and an anointed, albeit slowly growing, celebration/teaching event, compared to other churches you are doing OK. The average church in Britain is around 125 people. (It is a little less or a little more depending on whether you are charismatic or non-charismatic, evangelical or liberal.) However, if you are a church like my own of some 600 people comparisons are odious. There is a minimum of 75,000 people living in homes in the area we are working in. If Christ's will is that 'all' should be saved, we should not settle for any less. Most churches have never shared the gospel in any form with all individuals, households and people groups in their area. We are not doing all right!

4. We tried that once before

Having a go at something, such as prayer, evangelism or cell groups, is not good enough. The vision must be matched with a mission, and the mission has to encompass all ages within the church and allow for change. There has to be a long-term commitment to the elements of mission that includes prayer, evangelisation and social action. We sometimes need to apologise for 'having a go' and moving on to something else when it didn't work. Anyway, just because we tried something before and it didn't work doesn't mean that we shouldn't try it again if it is biblical and pleases our Lord.

5. It will cost us too much

The fact is, it cost our Lord Jesus everything to redeem us and offer us a changed life, a future hope and an inheritance where we share his throne together. Discipleship isn't cheap. Grace may be free to us, but it was not free to Christ. If we are unprepared to reach the lost we can only pray that God will raise up another group of people in the locality who will pay the price. And he usually does!

6. It is not our responsibility

This is normally either believed secretly or communicated privately by those who are locked into a maintenance mentality. The 'God will save whom he will' brigade interestingly enough were not saved and converted through that mentality. Someone somewhere shared their faith, conducted a meeting, preached in the open air, wrote a booklet or passed it on. If it is not our responsibility to have a life-long mission to reach our world for Christ, in God's name whose is it?

7. Let's wait and see if it works

However frustrating it is, we can only work with those who want to work with us. Jesus spent plenty of time with Peter, James and John, but it is never recorded that he spent any time on his own with Thomas or Judas. That is not to say he didn't, but it is interesting that Scripture records that he spent a lot of time with those who were with him and wanted to be discipled by him. We must work with those who want to follow us, embrace the vision, fulfil the mission and (as we shall see in the next chapter) pay the price. Whenever a shepherd wants to move on, those sheep that are nearest follow immediately. The main bulk eventually realise something is going on and get up and follow. But there are always a few that like it where they are and are threatened by the journey or unknown pastures. We cannot be responsible for them, but we can be an example of love, care and grace to them.

So much for my seven hindrances. Now we come to communicating the mission.

Mission and communication

According to Ravi Zacharias, there are four ingredients in all good communication. We see these expressed in the Godhead. We see them particularly expressed in the life and ministry of our Lord Jesus Christ. As the communicator par excellence, we would do well to learn from the God who communicates, the Son of God who communicates and the Spirit of God who takes these models of communication and imparts them to us in these latter years of the twentieth century.

Identification

Have you ever wondered why it was that God did not wait another 2,000 years before he sent his Son into the world? He could have reached the entire globe through satellite and cable television; through literature and videos; through radio and other means.

I will tell you why. While we should be thankful for most opportunities on national radio and television, as well as local stations, to share our faith and the fruit of that faith, we will never ever turn our nations round to God through television and radio. Television invites us to observe and at the most send our money in for the message. Christ on the other hand invites us to disciple-ship, into a local body of believers, the church! There one finds encouragement, prayer, teaching, checks and balances and a development of ministry. This cannot be done through television, particularly when it is geared to one man or woman and their ministry. Team ministry as seen in the Godhead, or with Jesus and his disciples and apostolic team, is virtually non-existent in television.

Christ came 2,000 years ago and identified with the people of his day and offered an invitation to disciple-ship. This meant something more than believing in God and sending in their money. Following Jesus meant associating with lepers and crooked tax inspectors, forsaking family and home, living by faith and kissing goodbye to a career. While that may not have been true for all disciples, Christ modelled something to those in regular employment which allowed them to embrace his vision and values, even though they may not have travelled with him.

So Christ, in order to reach his world, identified with it. Christianity is incarnational. Although this word does not appear in Scripture it expresses the meaning of Scripture. The eternal 'Word' became flesh (Jn 1:14). Christ came in the appearance of 'sinful flesh' (Rom 8:3). Right at the heart of our historic faith is the statement that there is a mystery of godliness. He 'appeared in a body' (1 Tim 3:16).

Incarnation does not mean that Christ was not God and was simply appearing as a man. He is a man. But he is not only a man. He did not exchange divinity for humanity. Rather he assumed humanity while retaining his divinity. He is both human and divine, and stepped into the world of time and space so that people could see what God is like, who God is like and how he acts to friends and enemies. Our Christianity must identify with those we are endeavouring to reach. In other words it must be incarnational.

Translation

Our faith must not only identify with the people groups we are endeavouring to reach, whether they be male or female, young or old, black, brown, white or yellow. Our message must also translate in a language that they (not simply we) can understand.

I have heard many messages and seen the Christian faith modelled in many commendable ways. The difficulty is, it just did not translate into language that the unchurched, uninitiated and unconverted could understand.

There is of course an anointing and the presence of God on certain lives which defies logic. I once heard Billy Graham speak at an evangelistic meeting at Earl's Court in London on 'The High Priesthood of Melchizedek'! The unchurched didn't have a clue who Melchizedek was, but more people responded that Thursday night than during any other in the entire crusade!

However, generally speaking, people cannot commit themselves to things they do not understand. Therefore the language of love and grace, and truth and final judgement must be translated into a language they can understand.

People waving banners around in the High Street and shouting in a spirit of hostility against sin may produce an accurate assessment of humanity's need, but it does not translate easily! People are put off before they have even heard the message. Hostile, sin-centred street preaching does not make Christ attractive or intelligible. In my Plymouth Brethren days, I asked our elders why so few ever came to Christ. I was told that we had at one time delivered a tract to every household. 'They will never be able to say they never knew,' was the response I received. Translating the gospel into a language the unchurched can understand was nowhere in their thinking. 'Getting our message across' was only seen from 'our' point of view.

Persuasion

Identifying with those we are endeavouring to reach (instead of preaching at them), and translating the message in a language they can understand is vital.

But quite often, sensitive people are not very persuasive when endeavouring to communicate. Out of a fear that persuasive language may appear to be manipulative, there is often an absence of persuasiveness in our communication.

We communicate at various levels. When in conversation over the dinner table one look from my wife can tell me I am sharing too much with the wrong person! She has communicated without a word being spoken. Her looks have often saved me from embarrassing situations.

A consistent life is another very persuasive force. Mother Teresa's care for the poor has been a persuasive force throughout the world. Dr Billy Graham's evangelistic ministry, conducted while he was in his 70s and well after his fiftieth wedding anniversary, has been another persuasive force. The untold and unheralded acts of Christians in almost every locality have often been the most persuasive elements in keeping us on course as disciples of Christ.

When towards the end of his life Paul was asked to give a defence of his faith, King Agrippa said to him, 'Do you think that in such a short time you can persuade me to become a Christian?' (Acts 26:28). The Bible is silent as to whether or not Agrippa was being cynical or genuinely sincere. But Paul certainly was a very persuasive man with thousands of believers and sizable churches to his credit.

One of the reasons many so-called clergy are not persuasive on the platform or in the pulpit is because they have forgotten all biblical principles over which we should be persuasive. But apart from principle we should ask the Lord to make our voices so like his own that all those who are seeking meaning to life will recognise the voice of the Creator and Redeemer and follow him.

Justification

Identification, translation and persuasion are three vital elements in all good communication. But there will come a time when we are asked to justify why what we are saying is so important as against what the Muslims, Hindus, atheists or agnostics are saying.

Shortly after being healed by Christ, an ex-blind man was able to say that although he didn't know whether Jesus was the Son of God, he could say, 'Once I was blind but now I see.'

That is a brilliant, effective and accurate story. It is fine shortly after one has been blessed by such a miracle. Little more can be expected. But it is not good enough for a disciple of years' standing simply to say, 'My God heals.' We must also be able to justify the importance of what we are saying.

If we cannot objectively justify why our message is unique, and therefore more important than anybody else's, we shall be lost in a sea of subjectivity we may never get out of.

Truth on the airwaves

On a live radio programme in the South of England, I was confronted by an atheistic professor. 'You Evangelicals,' he hissed. 'You and your truth, your absolutes. There is nothing absolutely right or absolutely wrong.' Quickly drawing on something I had heard before, I responded, 'If that's true, you can't be absolutely sure about that!' That was the end of the debate!

On another occasion I was challenged, 'You

Evangelicals—all you are into is brainwashing.' I responded, 'That is a very astute observation,' and paused. 'The only difference between godless humanists, which you represent, and Christians, which I represent, is that what we are washing our brains in is a lot cleaner than what you are washing your brains in!' The idea that you can walk through this world without having your brain affected by the media, advertising and peer pressure is ludicrous. The question is, 'What are we washing our brains in?'

We do not have to throw our brains away in order to become Christians. Quite the reverse. It has been said that conservative Evangelicals are dead from the neck down, while charismatics and Pentecostals are dead from the neck up! It is important that with sound mind and moved heart we are able to justify why we believe what we believe in as many ways as possible. Reading Scripture and good books about Scripture is vital, alongside the tapes we listen to which are either motivational or full of wonderful stories. God will extend grace to nations with a high rate of illiteracy, though they are unlikely to be asked to justify, from an academic or objective point of view, why they believe what they believe. But I am not so sure God will extend the same sort of grace to those of us whose mission has been impaired through an unwillingness to learn from others regarding our faith and how it relates to the complex world in which we live.

A global mission

If our vision is to see our globe networked with the gospel, it stands to reason that we must start networking the area in which we live. The worst sort of

Christianity is that which wishes to be good news to people who live 3,000 miles away, but is non-news at best, or bad news at worst to those who live 300 metres away.

In 1885, D.L. Moody and A.T. Pierson had a vision to complete world evangelisation within fifteen years. That vision led to a mission, a journey with a purpose, in which they were defeated.

Ten years later A.T. Pierson explained, 'We are compelled to abandon the hope.' The vision was a biblical vision, but for numerous reasons the journey with a purpose was not fulfilled.

Was it because of a failure to understand that such a mission would demand a marathon rather than a short sprint?

In 1910 the Edinburgh Conference was held, bringing together Christians from many nations. They also recaptured the vision for worldwide evangelisation in their generation. Some say the reason they failed was identical to the reasons Moody and Pierson failed. Others would add that the International Missionary Council suffered liberal influences which led to maintenance orientation and a lack of concern about mission which led to the World Council of Churches.

One thing is clear: conferences led, planned and addressed by non-practitioners will never see the vision become a fully-fledged, long-term mission.

One of the great cries of church leaders everywhere is 'how' rather than 'what'.

Today it is reckoned there are around 550 million disciples of Christ. The unevangelised population, including so-called nominal Christians, is close to 5 billion people. In mathematical terms it simply means that each one who is a true disciple of Christ need only reach ten people and world evangelisation would be completed.

While it is regarded that these latter years of the twentieth century will give us unparalleled opportunities, it is also regarded that it will be a time of unmatched opposition. We come to that issue in the next chapter.

But *how* do we network an area or a people group?

1. Evaluation

How many people live in your area? What sort of people are they? Black, brown, white, yellow or a mixture? Are the people rich or poor or middle class? Is there a youth culture and how are they serviced by the local council and education? What about older people, a growing section of society? Where are they and how are they catered for? It is hopeless enthusing teenagers and young adults with reaching the next town with the gospel when it is a retirement town for over sixty-fives!

2. Reporting

When the situation has been evaluated, we need a reporting facility. Those carrying the burden for an area are unlikely to be simply the clergy or full-time elders and those in apostolic and prophetic ministry. The evaluation must be reported back, not only to overseers, but to practitioners who will do something about the reports they are receiving. Without a proper report-back forum the burden will be carried by too few or inadequately spread among too many.

3. Selection

On the basis that we cannot do everything at the same time, we have to select people to prayerfully, practically, lovingly and sensitively target people groups in the area. If we target children at school and young adults at secondary school, college or university, Sunday meetings using the Authorised Version and singing hymns accompanied by a clapped-out or reconditioned organ may not be the best way of making disciples! Equally, if we are going to target sensitively those in their fifties, sixties and above, happy, clappy soft rock music may not be the best church meeting to bring them into—particularly if they listen to a classical music radio station. They are certainly unlikely to know the latest Michael Jackson single or Take That offering!˙

4. Discipleship

In any mission work, the majority of work goes into evaluating, reporting and even selecting. Little goes into the issues of follow-up, discipleship and changing whatever needs to be changed in church structures to accommodate the steady trickle or stream, never mind a river of converts. One-to-one discipleship and special cell groups to facilitate teaching, instruction and participation are vital—alongside regular church meetings. If we do not know how to disciple people into the ways of God we will always fail in our mission to evangelise our locality or area with the gospel.

Discipleship is bringing people to a place where they themselves will then prayerfully and sensitively take the good news of Christ to their own people groups, so that we are in a reproductive situation.

What of today?

Billy Graham and Luis Bush of the AD 2000 Movement have challenged Christians with a vision and a mission.

'A church for every people and the gospel for every person—by the year AD 2000.' The world evangelised by the year 2000. Is it possible?

Thank God his purposes are corporate and not individual. This mission can only be done as we submit ourselves to Scripture, the Holy Spirit and to one another in the love, joy and fear of the Lord. A community of faith will give us a clue as to the age to come. Our individualist culture must be abandoned. We belong to a church embracing relationships, partnership and co-operation, without which we will never fulfil the vision.

To all evangelists I would like to say that we cannot separate New Testament Christianity from the church, local and international. Evangelism, engaged in to the exclusion of fellowship, worship and discipleship, will not produce a new order, a new society to usher in the new age. Chuck Colson has rightly said that we cannot separate the nature or character of the church from its task.

God does not want us to live with a mission formed by default. He has something in mind for us, which is more than being reactive to the needs around us and being absorbed into maintaining church, important though that is. It is a journey of faith, involving failure as well as success, and he has made provision for both. It is directly related to the cost we are willing to pay to see God's kingdom come and will done in our world, geographically and relationally.

3

Counting the Cost

The orgasm has replaced the Cross as a focus of longing and the image of fulfilment.

Malcolm Muggeridge

We are the music makers,
We are the dreamers of dreams,
Wandering by lone sea breakers,
And sitting by desolate streams;
World losers and world forsakers,
On whom the pale moon gleams:
We are the movers and shakers of the
     world forever, it seems.

One man with a dream, at pleasure,
Shall go forth and conquer a crown;
And three with a new song's measure
Can trample a kingdom down.

For each age is a dream that is dying,
Or one that is coming to birth.
  Arthur William Edgar O'Shaughnessy (1844–1881)

Music making, dreaming dreams, conquering unchartered territory—this is the stuff of the visionary. But O'Shaughnessy's couplet to finish his remarkable piece of prose is worthy of another mention:

56

> For each age is a dream that is dying,
> Or one that is coming to birth.

Is it worth dreaming in such an evil age?

It could be argued that evil simply happens. But just as an uncared-for garden becomes chaotic and un-manageable, or an uncared-for engine will eventually break down, lack of moral standards leads to unruly growth and breakdown. It has been said that in order for evil to flourish, good people simply have to sit back and do nothing.

Each of us as individuals is the sum total of the decisions we have made. We may have had little influ-ence on some of our circumstances, but we are respon-sible for who we are, despite those circumstances. There are many things that are coming to birth simply by letting selfish, sectarian and heartless people choose to do their thing. And as far as cost is concerned, when evil flourishes it is nearly always the innocent who suffer.

For goodness, decency and righteousness to flourish a clear choice has to be taken. But the cost has to be counted, for only then will the full effect of the choice be realised. This is true of the parents who wish to give their child a good education, a special treat, or maybe a major present of a bicycle, a motor bike or even a car. It is a good, well-intentioned aspiration, but in order to turn that aspiration into an achievement, the cost factor must be weighed. For most parents these days (and in many cases we are talking of a single parent) such a gift might mean postponing a holiday for a year, no new clothes for twelve months or maybe taking on an extra job to earn the necessary income to buy the gift.

Counting the cost—development

People often ask me what the difference is between those filled with aspiration and achievers. The answer? Development! Countless aspirations are never realised because people are unwilling to develop the aspiration, pay the price and make it happen. The world is full of brilliant 'could have beens' who were unwilling to sacrifice in order to see the vision become reality.

Take the person with an ear for music, but who wouldn't practise daily on the piano, who has grown up always observing and listening but never participating. Or the person who wanted to influence groups small and large, those in the church and those outside of it, with oratory and passion. But that person never paid the price of listening to other speakers, sitting under fine oratory, overcoming public nerves, making mistakes and still pressing on to be a blessing to others. Others never overcame superior attitudes that can come across when endeavouring to teach or instruct and therefore they rarely got a hearing.

If individuals and communities were willing to pay the price, meet the cost, of good and noble aspirations, what a different place the world would be today. Perhaps your village, town or the area of the city in which you live would be different if you were willing to pay the price and meet the cost for your own aspirations to be turned to achievements.

Hope deferred

Jesus Christ, on one occasion recorded for us by Dr Luke, told the story of a person who had a vision to build a tower. He related that vision, directly and exclusively, to the issue of cost. If the cost has been miscalculated, it is easy to find that after laying the foundation one is unable to finish the task and then 'everyone who sees it will ridicule him'.

There is perhaps nothing worse than looking back over our lives and ridiculing our aspirations and the lack of fruit. Perhaps the one thing that *is* worse is others ridiculing us for having wasted so many opportunities, having squandered skills, time and resources and special opportunities. A writer of Proverbs commented, 'Hope deferred makes the heart sick, but desire fulfilled is a tree of life.'

You do not have to be a charismatic Evangelical in order to be fruitless or sick with hopelessness. However, I have observed as a charismatic Evangelical that it is more often than not charismatic Evangelicals who end up disappointed and disillusioned. Tongues and interpretation, prophetic promises of blessing and works of knowledge and wisdom, whether observed second hand or experienced first hand, are powerful tools to equip and focus our lives. However, it could be said that the less that is promised, the less likely there will be disappointment and hopelessness. Many Christians seem to survive and are fulfilled when leading quiet lives, fulfilling their jobs, whether at work or at home, caring for children, parents and relatives and generally being nice, co-operative, helpful people.

Please do not think I am being dismissive. The world would be a much happier place if every individual had faith in God and lived like that. Homes and businesses would become places of warmth, respect and co-operation. Such lives would raise the moral tone of just about every area of our existence.

But as I have often said, even Christ was not as nice as

most Christians. Being nice is not the end of the Spirit-filled life. For although there is the fruit of the Spirit, including love, patience and self-control, there are also the gifts of the Spirit. Paul lists these in different places and no one list is exhaustive. But being on the receiving end of an authentic prophetic word is, to my mind, awesome.

Post-charismatic depression comes when a person, or indeed an entire church, has lived with recently written songs, good Bible teaching and a strong prophetic call for the church to function as a body and reach out to the lost. But it all takes so long and costs so much! The depression is furthered when the prophetic is left to 'sort of happen'.

Misuse of promises and gifts

Having the inquisitive mind I do, I often wonder what would have happened if Samson hadn't had a soft spot for the ladies, and therefore hadn't lost his power. I often wonder what would have happened if Joseph had not foolishly shared his amazing dream with his brothers, parading his blessings around and causing jealousy. I wonder what would have happened to the Apostle Peter if he hadn't been so bound by Jewish legal tradition, causing him to be the reluctant evangelist in the house of Cornelius. Aspirations, dreams and visions and words from the Lord frittered away through negligence, sectarianism, pride and irresponsibility. Yes, God was glorified in the end, but I suggest it had more to do with the sovereignty of God than the original purpose of Samson's agreement not to drink alcohol or have his hair cut, Joseph's response to a dream or Peter's understanding of the gospel.

Post-charismatic depression comes when we have believed God's word in our hearts and minds as it comes through Scripture and prophecy, but we become unwilling to pay the price, or sacrifice whatever is necessary in order to see Scripture and the prophetic word fulfilled. The Apostle Peter had to overcome his prejudice and legalistic attitudes. Then he had to sacrifice his pride and knowledge of Jewish law in order to take the gospel to the Italian centurion Cornelius. He then had to sacrifice pride even further when going back to Jerusalem, the virtual headquarters of the church, to explain to born-again Jewish leaders that non-Jews had received salvation and were speaking in tongues and praising God without circumcision or walking in the law of God! It was staggering.

A sharp focus

I once counselled a teenager, who through circumstances of life and exposure to Scripture and prophetic ministry believed that God had his hand on his life in a special way. I agreed with that perspective. As a result he applied to go through the Pioneer TIE Teams (Training In Evangelism). This is a year-long course of theological study and practical work, which includes being seconded to churches to work alongside them in a wide range of evangelistic efforts. He grew in faith, usefulness and stature. At the beginning of the course he came to see me, explaining his aspirations. Having been pleased with what I heard I told him, 'It is important you forget about girlfriends for the next year or two. Give yourself to this course, to male friendship, to study and to travel.' He did so for precisely the duration of the course. I sometimes think (quite wrongly I am sure) that he walked out of the course when it finished and phoned a girl as soon as he got home. The girl was a lovely girl, but his focus was redirected. He spent all his time with her, and they even held hands in worship meetings! One can only hope that this was a temporary diversion. But usefulness (outside of the necessities of work) became minimal. For the time being, his training in theology and practice in evangelism had been wasted. He lost his focus, as he was not prepared to pay the cost involved in maintaining it. He is slowly finding that focus again.

Wasted fruitless sacrifice

The well-known proverb 'Where there is no vision, the people are unrestrained' (Prov 29:18, NASV) applies to more than the individual.

I have been around long enough to see people come to faith and experience the baptism in the Spirit, speaking in tongues and seeing divine intervention through prayer or healing. But so many of those people are in churches where the minister is not even born again, never mind filled with the Spirit. Scriptural platitudes cover unbelief. Religious gobbledygook hides the lack of a personal faith in Christ, a high view of Scripture or indeed faith in the gospel of repentance leading to forgiveness, restoration and a new beginning.

In some churches Universalism is taught (ie, we are all going to get to heaven in the end). In the age to come, Saddam Hussein is having tea with the Kurds he slaughtered. The religious, agnostic Serbians are apologising to the 20,000 Muslim women they raped. Madonna is no doubt giggling at her stage performances. The perpetrators of Tiananmen Square are shrugging their shoulders and smiling benignly as they bring to mind bodies crushed by tanks, students shot in the back of the head with a single bullet and Christian leaders imprisoned for decades, beaten, starved and tortured.

Do you know what? Born-again Christian believers put up with it all! Not only do they go along to such churches, praying for change and hoping for better things, but they actually put money into them to support their work and ideals. Dwindling attendances, and disenchantment among our own children regarding Christianity, do not deter them. They would rather sit it out for another ten or twenty years hoping for another minister, than acknowledge that this is not New Testament Christianity. This is a religion that recites the creed on Sundays, but believes something else on Mondays. It is a way of life that is a pleasant alternative to the nasty ways of the rest of the world, but it is not authentic Christianity. They would rather see their children grow up being turned off church for ever by religious drivel than pay the price, change churches and even move house to be a part of a body of people who love Christ and Scripture and who are unashamed in their devotion to both.

Movers and shakers

It was Albert Einstein who said of Christ, 'I am fascinated by this luminary from Nazareth. No myth could be so brim-full of life.'

Vision filled Christ's life. It was 'for the joy set before him' that he 'endured the cross, scorning its shame'. The cost and the shame of the cross were outweighed by the vision. The writer urges us to consider Christ, his life, death and resurrection, and the vision which kept him focused 'so that you will not grow weary and lose heart' (Heb 12:2–4).

Thank God there are plenty of people who are willing to make the move from aspiration to achievement, and are willing to shake off the weights that tie them down. As people focus on their own vision, and then submit their vision to local and national visionaries, an important development emerges.

Paying the price releases resources. The alternative to the one-man ministry is not an every-person ministry running around all over the place. After all, if the one-man ministry created a lethargic body, the every-person ministry will create chaos.

In any one church, there must be a visionary or a group of leaders who are linked to visionaries (apostles and prophets?) as a church can only have one vision. If a church has more than one vision it has division!

The Lord taught me a lesson here. I have always had a fascination with the media. I have been privileged to be the subject of a half-hour documentary on my own life and ministry which was extremely objective and favourable. I have appeared on scores of national and local radio and television programmes, often for no more than a few minutes. But I have had more than one significant prophecy, and words of encouragement from charismatic Evangelicals and non-charismatic Evangelicals, concerning my role in the media.

It is easy, if one wishes to be useful to Christ, to his people and to those who are not yet Christians, to see all of that become a self-centred motivation. *I* want to be the one on television. *I* want to be the one who is asked for my opinions on a wide range of things. *I* want to be the one who has a high profile or even the highest profile in the country. It is not that those things in and of themselves are wrong. Someone is likely to have the highest profile in the country, and it won't be the one who is happy to sit at home and be nothing and do nothing. Somebody needs to be on television speaking words of truth, life and faith. But I had to ask myself the question: 'Is the most important thing here that it is me who does it?'

Perhaps it won't be me in the way I thought it would be. I recall that so many who prophesied and received prophecies had not the first clue what they were prophesying about or what they meant. Few really understood that a virgin would conceive or that the Saviour would die upon a tree. They even had a theology for it: 'Cursed is everyone who hangs on a tree!'

It could be said, nearing the age of fifty-one, that this hope deferred causes discouragement and even, God forbid, the despising of prophetic ministry!

One morning, while sitting in the last session of Britain's National Evangelists' Conference, the well-known British evangelist Steve Chalke was bringing the breaking of bread meeting to a conclusion. Mentally I already had my hat and coat on. I was looking forward to seeing my wife, and wondering how much of a demolished rain forest was sitting on my desk. Out of the blue, without any warning, I received the most fantastic idea—that I should give a small microphone brooch, that I wore regularly, to Steve Chalke. I blinked with surprise. 'But this is the only one in the country,' I thought. 'I bought this in New Zealand. It reminds me of a very important incident, and it helps me pray for the people of New Zealand.' But I had learned through trial and error (a great deal of trial and not a little error) that this was the voice of the Holy Spirit.

When the meeting was over, I walked up to Steve, who was a good though not particularly close friend at the time, and I told him I had something important to say. I was extremely nervous and knew I could not explain the value and significance of giving away this little microphone brooch which probably cost me less than £1. So that there could be no confusion due to my nervousness, I asked another friend and colleague Stuart Pascal to witness what I was about to say. Stuart is a descendant of Blaize Pascal, the seventeenth-century mathematical prodigy, physicist, inventor and literary stylist, without a doubt one of the great minds of Western intellectualism. Falteringly, I explained the sentimental and spiritual value of this tiny brooch; that it meant a great deal to me (though I didn't go into detail), but that I felt I should now give it to him. I went on to say that I would be praying that he would become a voice to the nation, particularly through the medium of television. He listened intently, but other than a polite thank you he gave nothing away as to how he was feeling and what this all meant.

Paying the price, reaping the reward

Six months later Steve came to a prayer event I was leading in London, and we went out to supper afterwards. 'Got a story to tell you,' he smiled. What unfolded was nothing short of remarkable. A few days after receiving the brooch he had his car stolen. Being December, his vehicle happened to be filled with Christmas presents, his briefcase, diary, personal papers and his jacket with the microphone brooch attached. He explained how he was obviously very disappointed at the loss of the car and all his belongings, but particularly the microphone brooch. His wife Corni nodded in agreement. He then received a phone call from the police, who told him not to get too excited, but they had found one or two personal effects. He went to the police station to find his brief-case, completely empty of everything—except for the pin brooch! He told me, 'I just felt the Lord was saying to me, "There you are, Steve. When I give you a prophetic word, I will fulfil it. Nothing can take my promises away."' He concluded that within days, he was asked to do a ten- to fifteen-minute slot on British national television for a brand new, two-hour, thirteen-week series on Christianity! He went on to fulfil a regular slot on ITV's Breakfast Television for GMTV.

I could hardly contain myself. I was delighted, thrilled and privileged to play some small part in it. Freed from feeling I had to be at the centre of things, God's desire became the centre of my will. It no longer mattered who had the opportunities, the profile or the acclaim. What mattered was that Christian perspectives, views and reasons for faith were touching the lives of millions of people.

> For each age is a dream that is dying,
> Or one that is coming to birth.

Paying the price gives meaning

I consider my friend Ravi Zacharias to be one of the finest apologists of our time. He explained to me on one occasion that he had recently spoken to 500 top nuclear physicists and scientists in America. It was a sort of American think tank. He commented, 'You know, after-wards, not one of them asked a question about evolu-tion or science. Every single one had to do with whether or not we can discover meaning in life.' The search for significance, meaning and validity in our chaotic world occupies believers as well as unbelievers.

The book of Judges closes with some alarming words: 'Everyone did as he saw fit.' This was individualism, dissipating resources, failing to acknowledge proper leadership—the visionaries who had been mandated by God to shepherd and lead God's people. The writer of the book of Judges is not suggesting that those who were doing what was right in their own eyes were all evil. In fact, he gives us a clue as to why this was the case: 'Israel had no King.' Without leadership, everybody took their own initiative and no doubt went in a multiplicity of directions. Following visionaries demands laying aside our vision. The price involves submitting our personal vision for the corporate good.

Lack of corporate vision eventually produces tiredness. We are not going anywhere as a people. We don't have to be anywhere by any particular time. All of us have experienced how tiring it is sitting around reading the newspaper and drinking coffee on our days off. But individuals within any community, including the Christian community, can run around with their own agendas, their own vision, without leadership which, in the long term, also produces tiredness.

Why? Because we were made for one another—not simply for ourselves.

I have taught and lectured in several Bible colleges in the UK, continental Europe and the USA. Hardly any give attention to vision or team relationships to fulfil that vision. Many colleges create independency, and often isolate individuals, leaving them wide open to temptation which destroys or at best hinders the fulfilment of vision. Sin can cause failure.

Those who have failed, as they grow older, often become negative, disgruntled or, as G.K. Chesterton quipped, 'far from gruntled'. Sourness marks the response of such people when they hear of others who are doing well, achieving goals and fulfilling visions. We fail on our own and can grow old on our own. While the church is only as strong as each member, that strength is to be relationally blended into others' strength if it is to be of use.

As human beings we should go through three stages of life.

1. Dependency

This is of course the stage where we suck from our mother's breast or the feeding bottle. It is where we are washed, cleaned up, fed and carried around. We are utterly, totally and completely dependent on others.

Even Christ himself was dependent on his mother and father Joseph for the first few years of his life.

2. Independency

Generally speaking, within Christian circles independency is regarded as being immature, unspiritual and unco-operative.

However, it need not be so. Every individual, in order to know who he or she is and what they should be doing in life, has to be weaned away from dependency on others. There is something sad and pathetic about the grown up wife, husband or single adult who is still dependent on parental opinions, perspectives, whims and wishes. Independence from parents is a mark of growth. Decisions must be made without continual reference to others. Mistakes can be made and hopefully learned from. Successes are achieved and one is then able to receive congratulation and applause.

3. Interdependency

This is not the helpless dependency of the babe, nor the independent teenager or young adult flexing their new-found muscles.

This is something quite different. It has to do with knowing our gifts and skills, as well as our limitations and inadequacies; it is about functioning with a dependence on Christ and his word, and operating out of our own personality, albeit influenced by those we allow to influence us. It is, however, knowing we have blind spots, as well as an absence of skills and abilities which we are going to need if vision is going to be fulfilled through the cost of sacrifice.

The first thing our Lord did, having been filled and anointed with the Spirit, and having won victory over the powers of darkness, was to go out and choose a team of men he could work alongside as well as lead. They submitted to his vision and direction, but it was obvious they never felt crushed. They could make mistakes, again and again! They were not manipulated. Manipulated people know they cannot make mistakes. They live in fear and diffidence. It was Dennis Sawyer, a pastor in Seattle, Washington, who commented: 'The difference between manipulation and leadership is motive.'

Most people know more (intuitively) than they think they know. Good leadership is where the vision is outlined and repeated, and where room is given for individuals to absorb that vision. They can then bring their own skills and vision, and invest both into the overall vision in a specific ministry or locality.

To change the analogy, instead of individual trickles of water here and there, we can come together and create something far more wonderful: 'The day of the streams is over; the day of the river has begun.'

Vision is threatening

Paying the price may well release resources, and corporate vision may well give meaning if people are in churches where visionary leadership is accepted as the norm. But this momentum causes reaction. Don Marquis was right when he noted: 'If you make people think they are thinking, they will love you: but if you really make them think they will hate you.'

A God-given vision can be preached about, written about, passed on prophetically. But no person's revelation can be passed on in its entirety. The one thing you cannot give is the cost and sacrifice involved. That is why second and third generation disciples may say all the right words, but lack the heart, compassion and conviction of their former heroes.

The famous preacher in London's Westminster Chapel, Dr Martyn Lloyd-Jones, eventually left his cherished pulpit. Visiting many of the churches that followed his leadership, he made two interesting comments to a friend of mine. The first came after he had slipped into the back row of a number of Reformed evangelical churches: 'I didn't realise how boring church was till I sat at the back.'

The second comment came with a certain degree of sadness, having invested himself in so many of these leaders over so many years: 'These men are theorists.'

What did he mean? Simply that they had all the right words, their theology was probably faultless, they had read his books, and perhaps knew their Bibles well, but they had not paid the price. The sounds of sacrifice were missing.

As I was laughing and joking one day with a number of overseas preachers, one halted the entire proceedings with a most astounding statement. He remarked somewhat inquisitively, 'You must have suffered a great deal to have developed a sense of humour like that.' I was stunned into silence. I didn't consider myself as one who had suffered, particularly when one looks at the plight of millions of homeless, hungry, orphaned, beaten and misused people throughout the world.

However, that phrase caused me to reflect on the loss of my mother and father twenty years ago through cancer, and the loss of two of my very best friends when I could no longer walk with them, their vision and values. I thought of the sacrifice involved in being away from home, resisting temptation, confessing failures and making public mistakes.

The good leader must not only be willing to sacrifice and pay a price, but he must allow those following him to do the same. That makes people think, 'Do I really want to pay this price to achieve this goal?'

The church I lead in Surrey has been built on an Antioch model. We have trained up, produced and released a wide range of leaders, speakers, musicians and worship leaders. We have planted churches in Farnham and Molesey/Hampton Court in Surrey. People sold houses and moved into South West London to church plant in Tooting, Wandsworth, Putney and Balham. Antioch was the church that sent out Paul and Barnabas and many others. We learned that the only way to grow was to give our best away, and we are grateful for the privilege.

But of late, through a number of influences, we have begun to alter the model to an Ephesian model. The letter to the Ephesians not only covered the city, but many other villages that surrounded Ephesus. It was a large, thriving and healthy church. We realised that as well as giving many people away to half a dozen other locations, we needed to build up our own work that would support and sustain national ministries. We began to have a vision of a church of thousands, with a large facility in which we would meet—the complete opposite of small units meeting in hired halls, which was a good model that had served us up to now. People had grown used to being in a church of 300 people which gave others away, reached a similar number and then gave more away. Questions were asked, such as: 'How would I fare in a church of 3,000?' It was threatening. Fears bombarded people. 'Perhaps I will feel insignificant and a nobody in a group of 3,000, whereas in a few hundred I can be a somebody.'

We then decided to take up two separate offerings to collect money for this 'new facility'. Mature Christians who had been with us for years evaporated for no known reason. Others fogged the issue, saying that they couldn't cope or that they disagreed with the vision. Some days I laughed. Disagreed with the vision of reaching the lost, of covering every home and business institution with the gospel over and over again? How can any sensible Christian disagree with that? But there was a cost involved. It had to do with money. They weren't prepared to pay the price. Thankfully, through love, friendship and their own integrity some are returning and paying a price to do so. It was very difficult for me. I wanted to let them off the hook, pay the price myself. But I had to learn that every believer has to pay the price to see the corporate vision fulfilled, even as they live their own.

The Ephesian model had resident apostles and prophets operating out of a large church. Paul stayed in Ephesus for two years and with his team covered a wide area. It was the principal city of the Roman province of Asia, dedicated to Artemis (Latin Diana) who was regarded as the mother of all gods. At its peak it could have had as many as half a million residents. We looked at the area we were working in, enlarged it and asked the Lord to give us a fresh heart for the lost. It was a costly exercise as leadership structures were changed, roles redefined and people relocated to soak the area we were working in with clusters of prayer groups that would reach out to the lost.

So if you want to discover the sceptical, the fearful, the anxious and the hedonistic—find a vision. You will be surprised at the outcome, particularly when the issue of cost emerges.

Vision pursued creates change.

Investing in the vision means investing in people. It is then we find out whether they are rock or sponge. Disappointment with others—disillusionment when we find a divided heart rather than a focused mind— is all part of a cost, whether we are giving overall leadership of a church, or ministry, or a special people group within a given location such as youth, children or the arts. Counting the cost to fulfil the vision is a vital part of nurturing a dream 'that is coming to birth'.

Dream your dreams. Choose for Christ amid the darkness. Count the cost. Be prepared for hope deferred. Own up when you get things wrong. Maintain focus. Do it together—become interdependent.

Pay the price and make it happen. You'll shape the church!

4

Shaping the Church

The church exists for the sake of those outside it.
Archbishop William Temple

Our mission will move us to the fulfilment of our vision to reach the world, or our world, for Christ. It is a vision to live for. But there is a cost involved in being a disciple and making disciples of others. This brings us to the church—where disciples are developed. Discipleship is costly and it must come before everything else. Lack of biblical discipleship, or attention to it, will shape the church.

There are many things good and bad that can shape a church.

1. Tradition need not be old

The church shapes disciples and this is often the main source of influence. While this is obviously true of so-called historic churches with their liturgy, changeless styles and predictability, it is also true of newer, independent churches. By that I mean those who sing recently written songs (often and wrongly called choruses—choruses belong to the end of hymn verses!).

Tradition does not need 125 years to form. It need not

even take 125 months! Go to most charismatic independent or networked churches and you will find a lengthy time of worship, led by a soft rock band or classical group, followed by a talk lasting thirty-five to fifty minutes and either an appeal or closing song. You can pretty well count on the immortal words, 'I know we have gone over time, but just before we go we'll sing song number . . . !'

Not all tradition is bad. Giving thanks for a meal, having an opportunity to pray with people after a meeting, singing songs of worship when together, reading Scripture publicly, and praying with children before they go to sleep are all good traditions. They need not be slavishly adhered to, even if performed regularly, as with birthdays, Christmas and holidays. These are familiar landmarks that help people celebrate, gauge progress and feel useful.

But not all traditions are good either. Singing in Shakespearean language or reading from the Authorised Version is great for the initiated who love such rich tradition. Only a fool would fail to acknowledge the precious doctrines contained within seventeenth- and eighteenth-century hymns, and it also has to be said that the literary language of the Authorised Version far outweighs many of the new versions. But when it comes to reaching out to the vast majority of people in any given locality, the unchurched, Shakespearean language will be a hindrance to all but the most educated. People, I find, put up with 'Ye' at Christmas while singing carols, but they won't put up with it for the rest of the year.

It is therefore important that we question our traditions—not with carping criticism, but in order to be constructive. Somebody once challenged me publicly

and somewhat loudly with: 'Why do you leave your
eyes open when you pray?' I replied, 'How do you
know that?' Strangely enough, to some at least, there
is nothing in Scripture that says you must close your
eyes when you pray, bow your head before you eat a
McDonald's hamburger, read your Bible every morning,
have a quiet time, or go to church on a Sunday. These are
traditions. Robert M. Brown commented: 'Does Protes-
tantism have a heritage of worship? . . . Yes, although
this does not imply doing things in church "just because
the Reformed do". Calvin wore a hat in church . . .
Because the church had (a) draughts and (b) pigeons.'

2. Crisis need not be disastrous

Having a vision and paying the price can create individual and corporate crisis. It can cause a crisis of faith in
Scripture, and challenge the vision itself. When things
go wrong we can lose faith in Christ and his vision.

Paul was in prison, but there wasn't the earthquake or
angels which accompanied Peter's prison experience. So
was this crisis a time for Paul to gripe? No. Why?
Because he had already counted the cost of the vision
he embraced when he realised that the process of attaining the goal would lead to a 'critical mass' of opportunity and opposition.

These are undoubtedly years of unlimited opportunity. They are also years of unparalleled opposition.
Such a clash produces crisis.

Vision should not be the result of mere discussion and
brainstorming. But if a vision is going to work, it must
spread from the visionary to be discussed, brainstormed
and owned. The Day of Pentecost was preceded by a
time of prayer, discussion and no doubt questioning.

Those largely uneducated disciples had been with Jesus of Nazareth for three years or more, performing miracles where thousands were fed with a handful of food, the sick were healed and even the dead were raised. Into those heady times came an arrest, crucifixion and death. The disciples were afraid and in hiding, and Jesus Christ appeared to them, sharing food with them. In what seems no time at all some of the disciples stood with Christ until he was 'taken up before their very eyes, and a cloud hid him from their sight'. As he ascended they stared intently into the sky, while two angels asked them, 'Men of Galilee, why do you stand here looking into the sky? This same Jesus, who has been taken from you into heaven, will come back in the same way you have seen him go into heaven' (Acts 1:9–11).

Imagine what it must have been like for those disciples. Miracles were followed by the brutality of crucifixion. Death was followed by an astonishing resurrection, accompanied by angelic visitations. Some ran around terrified. Others locked themselves away. A few were in disbelief. Then, there they stood watching Christ ascend into heaven while they were being addressed by angels. If I had been one of those disciples, my emotions would have been those of a person on a roller-coaster who couldn't get off!

Crisis follows crisis. You cannot tell much about a person or a church when they are in answered prayer or obvious blessing. But you can tell a lot about a person or a church when that blessing seems to have dissipated, the word of the Lord is not flowing, prayers seem not to be answered and things appear not to be going according to plan. It is then, and only then, that you can really tell how much of the King and the kingdom is in that life or church. Do they still walk with God, and allow the crises to shape them to serve God in the future, in better days? Or do they retire hurt, gossip and complain, or turn to more specific, odious sin?

Holiness lies not in the emotions but the will. A church's commitment to Christ will be tested in such times. All good craftsmen test their materials. A whole church may be tested.

We should also remember that almost every 'you' we read in Scripture is a corporate you and not an individual one. Having the Scriptures in our own language and reading them for ourselves we can often make the mistake that Christ's purposes are simply with individuals. But when Peter wrote his first letter it was to thousands of Christians throughout Galatia, Pontus, Asia and beyond. They had suffered 'grief in all kinds of trials' and temptations. But Peter adds that 'your faith—of greater worth than gold, which perishes even though refined by fire—may be proved genuine and may result in praise, glory and honour when Jesus Christ is revealed' (1 Pet 1:6–7).

The reason for vision is to create a future.

The reason God allows crises is at least in part so that materials that have a future can be tested. We should never forget that we are here but for a 'moment', for in the vast sea of eternity, our few score years will be as a 'moment'. It is what we do with our moment that will determine our destiny. And it is often in moments of crisis we turn to God or turn our back on him.

An individual or church crisis takes us through the school of learning. Such a school may seem like an inescapable box—but it has tomorrow inside!

3. Scripture need not be boring

Some may be surprised that I have listed Scripture third. However, I am not implying that Scripture is less important than tradition or crisis! What a thought! What I am endeavouring to do is face facts. Most people are Baptist, Methodist, Anglican or independent, not through Scripture but through tradition or crisis.

The tradition may simply have been that our parents were Baptist and that is why we are. Alternatively, a crisis may have occurred in the family and one way or another we find ourselves in church. A while back a group of miners had been trapped in a roof fall, half a mile down a coal pit in Nottingham, England. The news bulletin one night stated: 'The pubs were empty but the churches were full.' Who wants to drink when members of one's own community are lying crushed and possibly asphyxiated half a mile under where you are munching crisps and downing pints? It is a time for prayer, to look for hope, and it was noteworthy that that mining community packed church buildings for that experience.

There are 22,000 denominations in the world and they grow in number daily. When it comes to Scripture, people see things differently on a wide range of issues, from women in leadership and ministry, through to styles of leadership and evangelism. When it comes to structure and accountability, some are footloose, fancy free and accountable to no one. Others are groaning under a mighty weight of accumulated bureaucracy. Scripture gives us principles, not only about individual lives, but also about the church. In fact it is clear that there are a number of models of church—of style and emphasis—even in the New Testament. Principle must be embodied in personality, and Bill Hybels is going to do it differently from John Stott; Ray McCauley is going to do it differently from David Yonggi Cho.

We live in a complex and complicated world. Many individuals and families are endeavouring to simplify their lives. Some are ticking the little boxes on Visa or American Express literature stating they don't want to be receiving literature from other companies. Some I know have actually sent back many of their credit cards to simplify spending, to monitor the budget more easily, to save time in paying bills and reading literature and to minimise things that can go wrong.

When it comes to the church, we have to face the fact that there is now a wide range of speakers, styles and public meetings, and a plethora of books, tapes and videos. It is clear that God is blessing individuals and groups who don't believe what we believe or do things the way we do. We like to simplify things.

Does it matter?

There is the ever present tendency to assume it does not matter what you believe or how you behave. A well-known journalist recently gave a speech castigating a Christian organisation for refusing to have a speaker who divorced his wife and married someone else. To be sure, Christ expressed compassion and forgiveness to many wrongdoers. But most, if not all of these, were not practising believers. Jesus identifies with the wrongdoers, the powerless and the disenfranchised.

However, when it comes to Christian believers—those who claim to have been disciples of Christ—we move on from compassion and mercy to responsibility. If the

Christian organisation concerned was harsh and uncaring in its rejection of a certain speaker because of his divorce and remarriage (he left his wife), that is one thing. But I can only imagine, knowing them as I do, that a great deal of heart-searching went on in the light of Jesus' attitude to such people on the one hand, and signals that we send out, particularly to young impressionable minds, on the other. There are times when Christians sound more like the Pharisees than caring shepherds, but we are also in danger of sending out another set of signals which suggests that it doesn't really matter what you believe, and it really doesn't matter how you behave. God is blessing all sorts of people these days, no matter what they believe, and all sorts of lives, no matter how they behave. Scriptural models are rendered obsolete. Discipline is merely a personal thing which one may choose to follow, but there can be no corporate discipline. Like all liberalism, this, at its heart, has a death wish.

Jesus' best friend, John, said of his Master that he saw the glory of God in Christ 'full of grace and truth'. Some of us are full of grace, but in certain situations truth is a disposable commodity.

Others of us are firm on truth, but lack the effort and grace Christ showed in a wide range of situations. It was William Blake who wrote:

> A truth that is told with bad intent,
> Beats all the lies you can invent.

Given these complexities, some suggest it does not matter what we call ourselves as Christians. Herein lies a problem. I watch the news, and to my horror hear that a dozen school children and parents have been machine-gunned in Beirut. Who did this terrible thing? The Christian Militia. Now that is the sort of Christianity I don't want to be involved in.

What's your name?

Or I hear that a liberal Episcopalian bishop is not only approving of practising homosexuality, but virtually marrying two men in church services. Now I have a great heart for the homosexual and those battling with strong temptations towards their own sex, but in the light of Scripture, that cannot lead me to conclude that just because a person is tempted in a certain way we should accommodate it. So I do not wish to be identified with the Christian liberal who is blue pencilling massive chunks of the New Testament to accommodate his own moral weakness and floppy theology.

So we now come to the issue of what we call ourselves and others. Is it important?

Ask the mother, who failed to label the poisons in her medicine chest and consequently watches her son being raced off to hospital. Question the labourer, who failed to read the instructions when wiring the electrical appliance and now lies in hospital with third-degree burns.

Does it matter whether we call ourselves charismatics or Evangelicals? In the USA Evangelicals are seen as strong in doctrine, light on experience and often boring. It is assumed that evangelical churches are OK if you are pretty well educated, white and middle class. However, the Evangelicals view charismatics as strong in passion and zeal, but light on understanding and truth. When Benny Hinn was asked about the Trinity on national television, he replied that there are nine of them (a comment which he later apologised for), and Evangelicals either hung their heads in shame or roared with laughter! 'Blow on people and make them fall down under the Spirit, fine, but don't start talking about what the Bible says—you can't even count!' one said.

In Britain, you are either a conservative Evangelical (which normally means that you are non-charismatic or in extreme cases anti-charismatic) or a charismatic Evangelical.

To put it another way, my name is Gerald Coates. Primarily I am of the Coates family, but what marks me out as being different from my brother Roy or sister Miriam is that I am Gerald. But what unites us is the family name of Coates.

As a Christian, my family name is Evangelical. What I believe about Scripture, Jesus, the powers of darkness, heaven and hell, and the gospel determines how I live, what I preach and whom I work alongside. Little of that has to do with experience; most of that has to do with what I believe. There are all sorts of people who do things differently from me, partly due to tradition, skills and denominational upbringing. But I not only fellowship with them, I work with them, because they are primarily Evangelicals. John Stott, Michael Green, Colin Dye, Floyd McClung, Graham Kendrick, Tony Campolo, Cliff Richard, Ishmael and Reinhard Bonnke are some of those I have been privileged to work with. I don't share platforms with them based upon pentecostal experience, but upon what they believe regarding Christ, salvation and eternity.

I would find it difficult to share a platform of faith with the ex-Bishop of Durham, David Jenkins, who does not believe in the virgin birth, the physical resurrection of Christ or his physical return. His view of Scripture is so different from mine that in any given talk we would be in sharp disagreement to such a degree that it would undermine our whole message. For example, Jesus is either alive or he is not. Miracles either happened or they are just fantastic stories. Either Jesus is returning physically or we wait until we blow ourselves to smithereens or wipe each other out with 'pill and scalpel'.

As I have often said, we should not approach Scripture and say, 'Well, it's in the Bible, so I suppose it must be true.' Rather, we should approach the Bible in the knowledge of: 'This is true—that is why it is in the Bible.' Winston Churchill explained: 'Truth is incontrovertible. Panic may resent it; ignorance may deride it; malice may distort it; but there it is.'

Truth hurts at times, as we all know, but a painless world is not necessarily a good world.

There is of course no such thing as new truth. Somerset Maugham was right when he said, 'The great truths are too important to be new.'

Evangelical belief

So who are the Evangelicals? Where do they come from and what do they believe? You may find this interesting if up to now you have been satisfied to be known by your denominational tag or experience of the Holy Spirit.

Evangelical teaching comes from evangelical doctrine. We teach what we believe. Evangelical doctrine goes back to the first century of the Christian era, when creeds were put together to help people understand that a simple series of statements was what Christians believed.

Evangelicals affirm the following:

- The Bible is the truthful revelation of God, through which the life-giving voice of God speaks.
- God is the almighty Creator. We are his creation, and unlike all other life forms we were made in his image.
- God entered history to redeem humanity in the person of Jesus Christ.
- God's nature exists as three in one (God the Father, God the Son and God the Holy Spirit).
- Jesus Christ was born of a virgin, is fully divine and fully human without sin, died on the cross for all repentant wrongdoers, was buried, was raised physically to life and ascended into heaven.
- The judgement of sin is a reality for all humanity, but God has taken the initiative, through Jesus Christ by the Holy Spirit, to bring us good news.
- Jesus Christ will build his church as his followers seek the kingdom.
- The end of history as we know it will be expressed in the second coming of Jesus Christ, the general resurrection, final judgement, heaven and hell.

In other words, evangelical faith is traditional, orthodox faith.

Our function is to make Christ attractive and intelligible. Grace, mercy, forgiveness and friendship to others make Christ attractive. But how is he made intelligible? It is here that we must be able to justify the importance of our story. 'Once I was blind but now I see' is fine for someone who has just received a miracle. But as I have already noted it is an inadequate description of a disciple of Christ five years later. Following a person because they did a miracle for you is understandable at one level, but the supernatural is not limited to heaven, the Holy Spirit and angels. There are dark forces that will give you a miracle to ruin your life.

Any thinking agnostic has the right to ask, 'Why is your story, your faith, so important? Why is it more important than that of the Muslim, the Hindu or indeed the atheist?' We are bound to be asked, 'Isn't being kind, friendly and generous sufficient?' We need to be sure of the *facts*.

The believer's brain

In the emotionally charged film *JFK*, when investigations are being made years after Kennedy's murder, one investigator rushes into a room and proclaims, 'The President's brain is missing!' The issue of whether Kennedy was shot from the front or the back, from the grassy knoll or the warehouse, still occupies scores of writers. His brain was removed and preserved. What the American film-maker could not have known is that in Britain there is a satirical puppet-show called *Spitting Image*. President Reagan was presented as a head-and-shoulders puppet, and the top of his head was hinged. Each week, the top was lifted on the hinge and somebody would proclaim, 'The President's brain is missing!'—particularly after he had made a mistake in a speech or endorsed a crazy policy.

Living in the television age people switch on when they want to stop thinking. It is much more easy to be shaped by *EastEnders*, *Cheers!*, *Neighbours*, *Jurassic Park* or the plethora of chat shows or TV rock shows, so that we are, in the words of Neil Postman, 'amusing ourselves to death'.

Follow an imaginary but not unlikely conversation between a Christian and a colleague at school, university or work:

'Why are you a Christian?'

'Because Christ has forgiven me and made me a better person.'

'How do you know that?'

'Well he just has.'

'How do you know your change in behaviour can be attributed to Christ?'

'The Bible tells me so.'

'Why do you believe the Bible?'

'Because it is the word of God.'

'How do you know it is the word of God?'

'Well it just is.'

'On what basis do you say that?'

'Well, millions of people believe it!'

Is the Christian's brain missing?

Now the thinking person will not insensitively dismiss your new-found faith or optimism. Neither is he likely to disapprove of a life which is more loving, caring and sacrificial. What he will do is question whether all this is simply psychology, or whether you have any reason for suggesting that your faith is superior to others, and that the exclusive claims of Christianity are correct. That is why Scripture, books about Scripture and apologetics (the defence of the faith) are important. We may not all be academics—I am certainly not one myself—but if Christ, faith and discipleship are the most important things in life, they are worthy of more than mere agreement with what the pastor says, because he says it.

If we could see ourselves as others see us we would probably have our eyes examined! If we could hear ourselves as others hear us we would probably have our ears examined!

Many talk about the survival of the fittest in the rat

race of life. The glory of the gospel is that it transforms those of us who are unfit for anything other than mediocrity.

Perhaps one of the reasons we fail to reach out to others, making our faith attractive and intelligible, is because we are unsure of the reasons why we believe. Knowing in our heart is good and right. Knowing in our minds is something altogether different. The fact is, the church that is not reaching out is probably fading out.

The words of truth found in Scripture are not there simply to shape a life, but to shape the church and to shape nations. The church that is reaching out probably knows what it believes and why it believes it. Many of us need to stop talking for a while, and allow some thinking; perhaps some reading—Christian material that comes from another network or grouping than our own. Somebody once said, 'Thinking is when your mouth stays shut and your head keeps talking to yourself.'

I do not want historians to say of our time, and the church of our time, that it was more shaped by soap operas and television entertainers than by Scripture and the Holy Spirit.

4. Personality, leadership and ministry

There is a completely unbiblical idea, prevalent in many church networks, that human life and personality are at best debased. Unbiblical phrases such as 'Hide me behind the cross' and 'Don't applaud me, give the glory to Jesus' nurture this falsity. As human beings we are made in the image of God. The gospel gives us back our humanity. Sins are forgiven, hearts are exchanged, our minds are slowly renewed through Scripture and the Holy Spirit. However, as those created, we give honour and glory to God our Creator. But we dishonour God by saying that we are 'nothing', even though we may feel like that at times compared to his vast greatness and beauty.

Scripture and humanity

On almost every page in the New Testament we are encouraged to love one another, serve one another, respect one another, honour one another and think of others more highly than ourselves. When we rubbish ourselves it is a very short step away from rubbishing others.

When it comes to leadership, we are told not only to love, support and pray for them, but to give them 'double honour'. However difficult this may be for the Western mindset, this was written in the context of financial support. Put crudely, it means that we are to give leaders a double salary! Most Christian leaders I know are struggling on a less than average salary. There is also a mindset around that says, 'You keep the leaders humble, Lord, we will keep them poor!'

Jesus once told a remarkable story about new wine fermenting in skins. When the sweet juice was poured into the flexible wine skin, there was a great deal of effervescent activity! The skin would expand as the gas built up. But the skin became inflexible, and the point of the story is that unless you pour the fermented wine into another flexible skin, the original skin will break and you will lose the skin and the wine.

Many have explained that putting the new wine of the Holy Spirit (don't get drunk with wine . . . but be filled with the Spirit) into inflexible church structures will cause both the structure to be blown apart and the wine to be lost. Many leaders are happy when they are doing all the thinking and the congregation are doing all the agreeing. But once people are filled with the Spirit— truly filled—thinking and thanking go together. And voicing what they are thinking and thankful about soon follows.

Somebody once commented that the greatest danger the church can be exposed to is to believe that they have *methods* which cannot change, and a *message* which can!

It follows that shepherd leaders should be a few paces ahead of their sheep. To change the analogy, leadership should be more mature and more filled with the Spirit than those who look to them for leadership. Being a leader entails people looking at you, gaining confidence and watching how you react in situations both publicly and privately. In very many respects being a leader means being a role model for others.

The great debate in England regarding the monarchy, is that the total breakdown of so many marriages within the Royal Family means that they are no longer role models to the nation. The question is being asked, 'So why have them?' We have double standards here, of course: it is quite OK to commit adultery, providing you are not a member of the Royal Family or in national government. Even in post-Christian Britain, a person discovered in adultery, practising homosexuality or promiscuity is likely to lose office. But at least there are principles left which we can be hypocritical about. In so many situations, there are no such principles left.

Leadership qualification

A leader has been defined as someone who knows the

way, shows the way and goes the way. This applies to the cell group leader, youth leader, pastoral team or key player in a church.

In Christian terms, that is why we should never trust proud, self-seeking leadership. It is probably true that there are two kinds of leaders: those who want to do something and those who want to be something. Those who want to do something are to be trusted more than those who simply want to be something. But for the Christian, being precedes doing. We are called human beings not human doings.

So what are the leadership qualifications to shape a church properly?

- *Here for the long haul.* The skills it takes to gain office are not always the ones it takes to maintain office. Lives and churches aren't shaped in days or months, but years. We need leaders who are not using the church as a stepping stone for greater things. Rather, leadership should pay as much attention to what it is saying as it wants its listeners to when it comes to friendship, commitment and reaching out with long-term objectives.

- *An opportunist.* I appreciate this has a somewhat dismissive feel about it, but it is nearer biblical Christianity than the pessimist. The Christian is filled with hope and is looking for opportunities in every problem—not problems in every opportunity. Visionary leadership is looking for opportunities to share the gospel and pray for the needy; to bless rather than withhold blessing. Religious pluralism must be seen as an opportunity, though pluralism kills reality and destroys reason. The society we live in has largely become secularised, pluralised and privatised, and will end in a typical existential anticlimax. Wise leaders will surround themselves with those who are not afraid to ask questions, but it comes out of support rather than the tension of a different ethos of ministry.

- *Relationally networked.* Many Christians prefer to be spoilt by praise than saved by criticism. Leaders can be big fish in small pools. Relating beyond one's network and grouping creates health and security. It is always dangerous when leadership output exceeds input, especially when questions are likely to be asked about a style of leadership or the content of ministry. Relating beyond one's own congregation or network of like-minded leaders increases the opportunity for input from others, and acts as a healthy check and balance. A colleague of mine once said, 'This is the worst time in history for God to do something. We know it all!' Networking, relating to different people and sharing our faith, our ecclesiology and eschatology, often reveals how shallow and limited our understanding and perspectives are.

- *A kingdom person.* Jesus spoke of two things in his ministry. One was his Father in heaven; the other was God's kingdom on earth. Commitment to the kingdom must supersede commitment to denominations. ('Denominations' is an anagram for 'Not Made In Sion'!) Kingdom vision and values will mark the life of a Christian, who will in turn shape a section of the church to please the Master.

- *Servant leadership.* There is a tension between giving a clear, bold lead and acting as a servant of God and his people. The former can lead to domination, manipulation, control and a superior air. On the other hand, simply meeting people's needs erases all leadership. Christ washed feet, cooked breakfast and encouraged the discouraged among his own disciples. Yet he gave them a clear lead when it came to moral teaching and the issues of love and sacrifice. His servant leadership, I suggest, was the glue that held that band together for over three years.

Psychologists tell us that we have six basic needs, and the leader would be wise to note these. They are to be happy, to feel loved, to make an impact on our world, to find security, to experience significance and to be comfortable.

Nevertheless, biblical pastoral leadership is not running around simply meeting people's needs. That is a twentieth-century religious curse. The aim of pastoral ministry is not only to help people feel loved, to give them significance and all the other things I have mentioned, but to help them grow up. The role of pastoral ministry is first to be responsible for those who have not been responsible for themselves. Then to teach them responsibility, until they can be responsible for themselves. Ultimately, if they are to grow and be properly shaped, they must then assume responsibility for others. That is a mature church—one that has been shaped with good tradition, has come through crises, is allowing Scripture to impact every area of its existence and is following leadership that is making them more like Jesus.

It was Abraham Lincoln who rightly commented through bitter experience: 'You cannot help men permanently by doing for them what they could and should do for themselves.'

*   *   *

We have seen that vision leads us to mission. Mission helps us face the cost of our 'journey with a purpose'. Sacrifice leads us to discipleship and shaping the church.

But any believer who takes this seriously will not only please heaven, but will displease hell. So, what about the opposition?

5

Facing the Opposition

We have sustained a defeat—without a war.

Winston Churchill

Vision without a mission will turn sour.

A mission without counting the cost will be short-lived.

Counting the cost will involve reshaping the church at local and national levels. Everything we do in the church must be evaluated in the light of our goals.

Once the vision catches hold, the mission is underway, counting the cost has taken place and the price is being paid, opposition will persistently rear its ugly head. Any individual or group of people wanting to make heaven happy will make hell unhappy. While those of us who wish to please God and fulfil his word can expect the support of heaven, we should also expect opposition to come in many shapes and forms to hinder us from getting God's will done.

Religious opposition

The people of God cannot survive without absolutes. There are some things which, from God's perspective,

97

are absolutely right and other things that are absolutely wrong. Declare the former and you won't get into too much trouble. Declare the latter and you will be surprised at the opposition you get from other people who claim to be Christians. But the church cannot fulfil her mission without adhering to those absolutes, any more than a ship could fulfil its mission by celestial navigation if the stars were constantly shifting around.

After Jesus Christ had been baptised in water and filled with the Holy Spirit, he was tempted by the devil himself. The likes of us are not nearly important enough to be singled out for such specific temptation. The devil knew what he was up against in Jesus Christ.

Our temptations come in a much more subtle form. Even after our Lord had won the victory over Satan, he still faced opposition from the religious fundamentalists of the day. They believed in absolutes, but their absolutes not only included the law of God, but hundreds of other rules and laws which created a complicated network of legislation. If adhered to they made a person acceptable, but if deviated from they created marginalisation at best. The same God who gave the law to Moses kept the law in Jesus Christ, who was crucified by the Jewish community for one thing: 'We have a law, and according to that law he must die' (Jn 19:7).

They not only believed in the absolutes of God's law, but the absolutes of their own man-made laws. The two were so intertwined that the average innocent soul barely knew the difference between them.

Once we raise our heads above the parapet, if anybody in any locality dares to go public for the gospel, social action or church planting, we should not be surprised if they receive opposition from the religious status quo, whether it be quiet and undermining or otherwise.

Few of us are surprised if we receive hostile reactions from the parents of a young man or woman converted to Christ, or from those who have set themselves against God for one reason or another. They may be few and far between or, in some localities, thick on the ground, but anybody engaged in the gospel through words and deeds, as well as signs and wonders, should expect this opposition.

But what is often the most difficult to cope with, is opposition—a continual undermining—which takes place subtly, consistently and purposefully in the name of God and orthodox faith. In Jesus' day the perpetrators were called Pharisees.

Modern-day Pharisees

Who were the Pharisees?

These strict upholders of the law lost their political role once the Romans took control. Under Herod it was made clear that their influence must be purely spiritual. The Sadducees were their main rivals, who emphasised temple worship and taught in the synagogues.

Of high status among the Pharisees were the scribes, later called rabbis, and most were not professional full-time religious leaders. Josephus reckons that during Herod's reign they numbered around 6,000. They were a tight-knit community from which one could be expelled for non-conformity.

The popularity of the Pharisees was mainly due to their endeavour to interpret the law of Moses, with all of its strictness, with the needs of the poor in mind. The Sadducees, on the other hand, consisted of the most influential, priestly and aristocratic families. While the Jewish people were not necessarily disciples of the Pharisees, their strictness and apparent care for the poor were admired and applauded.

Nevertheless, Jesus of Nazareth seemed to be having continual run-ins with them. From the outset it seemed that Jesus refused to be limited by religious convention, and interpreted the law of God in the light of its original intention. This would have meant that synagogues, under the influence of the scribes and Pharisees, were closed to his preaching. Jesus became a controversial non-conformist.

So he found large crowds following him, gathering on hillside and lakeshore. Commissioning twelve disciples, together they announced the kingdom of God, which was accompanied by acts of mercy, power and deliverance. The crowds grew larger and more enthusiastic. There was the miraculous feeding of the 5,000, prayer time on a mountain, walking on the water and healing the sick.

And then—along came the Pharisees! Their first reaction was to Christ's disciples, eating bread with 'impure hands' that were unwashed. This was one of the 'traditions of the elders'.

Christ's response was staccato-like: 'These people honour me with their lips, but their hearts are far from me. They worship me in vain; their teachings are but rules taught by men' (Mk 7:6–7; quoting from Isaiah 29:13). Then he continued, 'You have let go of the commands of God and are holding on to the traditions of men.'

He then followed it through with a brilliant piece of observation and revelation: 'Nothing outside a man can make him "unclean" by going into him. Rather, it is

what comes out of a man that makes him "unclean"'
(v 15).

After more teaching, a demonic deliverance and a
healing, there was a further feeding of 4,000 people
this time. Then guess what? 'The Pharisees came and
began to question Jesus. To test him, they asked him for
a sign [or a testing miracle] from heaven' (Mk 8:11).
Later on the chief priests and scribes were endeavouring to 'take him out', as our American friends would
say. But they feared the crowds and so sent Pharisees to
'catch him' (Mk 12:13).

What on earth was going on here? These were religious people—they believed in absolutes—and Jesus
himself in this period was clearly teaching about fide-
lity, honesty, prayer and the Scriptures.

Two early heresies

Pharisees then and Pharisees today honour what God
has done, while strongly resisting what God *is* doing.
That sums up the whole Pharisaical mindset.

Compare, for example, the attitude which holds that
everything outside the hymn-prayer sandwich, occa-
sional, recently written songs and conservative non-
charismatic theology, is suspect, written off as gnosticism or deception. Pharisees rule OK.

Pharisees emphasise their correctness; their proper
and controlled style is adhered to in the name of reverence. (To revere somebody is to do what they want you
to do in the way they ask you to do it.) While emphasising Scripture, they only emphasise certain scriptures.
The psalmist's exhortation and even commandment
motivating us to shout, clap, dance and make a loud
noise is looked upon as being 'purely cultural'. Most

Pharisees are no better than liberals—they just blue-pencil different scriptures. Pentecost may be on their church calendar, but it is not in their corporate experience. Statisticians project that by the year AD 2000, the majority of Christians will belong to churches that have experienced the baptism in the Holy Spirit and the gifts of the Spirit as normal. But every great awakening will have its critics. The curse of religion lies thick upon many of our nations, and legalism lurks at the door if it hasn't already gained a massive foothold.

In first-century Christianity, two issues were regarded (and should have been regarded) as heresy. The first was Gnosticism and the second Pharisaism.

Gnostics held that the world was evil and the only things that mattered were spiritual. The very word 'Gnostic' comes from *gnosis* or ('knowledge'). So they went overboard on spiritual experiences, including prophecy and vision. But there seemed to be little discernment between the Holy Spirit and other spirits. Writers of the second-century church realised what a plague Gnosticism was. It became self-indulgent and unhinged from apostolic writings.

Simon Magus, recorded by Dr Luke in the eighth chapter of the Acts of the Apostles, is not described as Gnostic, but it is almost certain he was. He claimed to be divine and taught that salvation involved knowledge of himself.

The modern-day Pharisees regard prophecy, vision, tongues and such spiritual experiences as just another form of 'secret knowledge'. They believe charismatics are awash in a sea of subjectivity that will take us decades to get over. But what they may not realise is that alongside Gnosticism, Pharisaism was the second deadly killer. Hypocrisy, legalism and the reduction of

Scripture to mind-blowing nit-picking attracted Jesus' harshest comments. One of Jesus' disciples, Matthew, records Christ saying that 'the Pharisees sit in Moses' seat' (Mt 23:1). He went on to say, 'You must obey them and do everything they tell you' (I suggest because they were fairly correct theologically), but he added that they shouldn't follow their example in what they did.

What, then, was the main contention between Christ and the Pharisees?

Probably it was the relationship between the first five books of the Bible (the Torah) which contained 613 precepts, 365 being negative and 245 being positive. In Judaism there are no sacraments, and the rabbi conducts his affairs solely by virtue of his knowledge of the Torah.

The Talmud (sort of theological commentary) was valued by the Pharisees virtually as equal to the Torah. But Jesus abandoned such unscriptural belief and practice. As far as he was concerned the Torah was the word of God and the Talmud simply an interpretation, a commentary on the word.

Today, it could be likened to a Reformed Calvinist who treated Scripture and Calvin's writings virtually on an equal basis. Many would actually acknowledge that, for in reality that is precisely what the position is. To say that you are an orthodox Christian and an Arminian is, to them, tantamount to suggesting that you are as theologically astute as a cabbage.

Deliberately upsetting?

It is quite clear, in the later teachings of the Apostle Paul, that whenever he was confronted with a problem he erred on the side of grace and mercy. He never erred on the side of legalism and the sort of strictness that goes with it.

Jesus, prior to Paul's teachings, seemed to go out of his way to violate the 'traditions of the elders' on a fairly frequent basis. Having upset people in one synagogue, he then did a tour of them all!

Following Christ but preceding Paul, the Pharisees became so envious, hostile and suspicious of supernatural, spiritual happenings, that Peter and John could be hauled in front of the Sanhedrin with a simple question, 'By what power or in what name have you done this?' Why such a hostile attitude, when people were quite clearly being healed? I will tell you why. Because Peter and John were not part of the academic intelligentsia that made up the clerical Mafia!

In the autumn of 1993, I took part in a live one-hour BBC radio programme. The theme was 'Does God heal today, and how does the Christian community respond to such a claim?' Hosted by a most fair and professional interviewer, my opponent (for that is what he was) was Dr Peter May. He is renowned for telling audiences that in twenty-five years he has never found one single trace of a miracle. Dr Peter May put his views forward lucidly and succinctly: God can heal but, after twenty-five years of reading, researching and verifying, Dr May has never seen him perform a miracle or seen the results of a miracle. I for my part put forward the fact that God can heal and does heal, but if the same standards Dr May rigorously imposed upon people who claim to have been healed were imposed upon people Jesus healed, he would probably come to the same conclusion!

Interestingly enough, almost every person who phoned in to the radio station claimed to have had some sort of remarkable healing. All told their stories in a sane, sensible and cohesive fashion. One man phoned in to say he had been involved in a serious road accident and had been paralysed from the waist down. With only 20% feeling in his legs, he had gone off to a meeting and had been prayed for and was now completely healed and walking around normally. And Peter May's response? He explained that in the nineteenth century it was quite acceptable for people to walk around their homes quite normally but be taken out in wheelchairs to gain sympathy. Talk about 'believing the best' of one another! It was scandalous. But this is what the Pharisaical mind will do. Instead of, 'If that is true, it is a wonderful story,' which believes the best, but leaves room for verification, we get the opposite: 'I am not believing this until I have seen all the records and satisfied myself.' Verification, clarification and research should be welcomed rather than spurned, but listening to Dr Peter May, I realised he not only believes he has a handle on all miracles, but a handle on all doctors. One local GP phoned in to say that one of his patients had quite clearly been miraculously healed, and he had the records to show it. Dr May, simply a local GP himself, not an international medical genius on all health matters, explained he would want to see the records before he could accept that such a miracle had taken place. He, a local GP, didn't even believe another local GP. This is Pharisaism at its worst!

Educated into imbecility?

Members of the Sanhedrin were thrown off guard when they found that Christ's disciples were 'uneducated and untrained men' and began to 'recognise them as having been with Jesus'. But this was not a sentimental panacea greeted with smiling faces and knowing nods. Quite the opposite. They 'threatened them further'! It was inconceivable to the members of the Sanhedrin that people who had not been theologically trained could hear from God and do the works of God.

The Pharisees are not concerned with people who have been in wheelchairs for two years and are now walking around normally. Quite coincidentally (or was it providential sovereignty?) the man who had phoned our programme had been filmed by BBC Television after his accident. The programme had to do with the accessibility, or rather non-accessibility, of wheelchair users to shops and the like. Having heard him call the radio station, they filmed him again, walking around with a television reporter. God was glorified in ways that neither Peter May nor Gerald Coates could have conceived!

Root and fruit

The Pharisees showed up again after a blind man had been miraculously healed (Jn 9). But the Jews did not believe it, so they called in his parents. Afraid of what the Jewish leaders would do if they answered wrongly, they said, 'Ask him. He is of age; he will speak for himself.' The Pharisees charged the ex-blind man to 'give glory to God. We know this man [Jesus] is a sinner.' No doubt delirious that his groping around had now turned to seeing his intricate fingerprints and distant objects on the horizon he replied, 'Whether he is a sinner, I do not know; one thing I do know, that, whereas I was blind, now I see.'

But they wouldn't let go. How did he open your eyes? What did he do to you? One can hear the despair in the ex-blind man's response: 'I have told you already and you did not listen. Why do you want to hear it again? Do you want to become his disciples, too?' He could not possibly have imagined what that would stir up: 'You are this fellow's disciple! We are disciples of Moses! We know that God spoke to Moses, but as for this fellow, we don't even know where he comes from.' There you are! Credentials, theological training—if it is not in our book it doesn't count and we should know!

The Apostle Paul made an interesting comment in his well-known 'fruit of the Spirit' teaching. Listing the nine things that make up fruit of the Spirit he adds, 'Against such things there is no law' (Gal 5:24). Why add that? Because this assessment of testing someone's spirituality went against the nit-picking, by-the-book approach of the Pharisees, who reckoned that all phenomena, including healing, could be weighed and assessed through the Torah and the Talmud.

When Benny Hinn blows on people the response is, 'But it's not in the Bible!' When preachers pray for people and they are 'slain in the Spirit' the response is the same—'Where is it in the Scriptures?' But let me also ask, where is the one-man ministry? It is not there, yet God has worked through it none the less. Where is the hymn-prayer sandwich? Sunday schools? Ladies meetings? Six-thirty pm services? Church buildings? The gospel regularly preached to the converted? Bible studies which are exegeted line by line? The odd missionary or two sent out into a massive field of humanism or the demonic? You won't find much of this anywhere in the Scriptures. Yet this is regarded as orthodox Christianity!

The separation of emotions from reason is so uncharacteristic of Christ and of those who followed him and wrote Scripture. William De Artega has pointed out in his book *Quenching the Spirit*: 'For those who have watched the *Star Trek* series on TV we can see the result of this separation in the character of Mr Spock. That unfortunate hybrid creature cannot experience emotions and must make every decision on purely logical grounds.' Revival rarely, if ever, comes without a strong emotional response.

Revival or a great awakening?

Those who 'quench the Spirit' can do so in several ways. Some simply say or imply that the gifts of healing, tongues, interpretation and prophecy are not for today. Neither is the raising of hands or indeed any of the psalmist's injunctions to clap, kneel, shout or dance. It is unlikely that there will be many talks on 'the anointing' in these churches. To be sure, the Holy Spirit is often at work in such churches, particularly if the gospel is being preached and the word of God is honoured. But the Holy Spirit is severely limited, boxed in and boxed up. Mr Spock and company run the show. Logic reigns supreme.

Revival—biblical revival—involves both heart and mind. But most stories of Holy Spirit activity or revival seem to start with the emotions. Tears of repentance, falling on knees or face, loud prayers and songs, fiery preaching, hugs, kisses, even laughter. News from various parts of the globe tells us that laughter is an integral part of many church revivals that are going on. I predict that laughter is becoming one of the most controversial aspects of these days.

However, we must be clear that revival is not the answer to all of our twentieth-century dilemmas. In times past, in many parts of Europe and the USA, the majority of people were 'in church'. Revival *was* the answer to most of their dilemmas. Get the majority of the population revived towards God and one another, and it will affect the nations. Today only a small percentage of the population is committed to a Bible-believing, Spirit-anointed church. We need reviving—in faith and love, in the gifts of the Holy Spirit and in a growing burden for the lost. But we are in a tiny minority.

Ultimately what we need is not revival but a great awakening. Revival is for the church. At least there is something there to be revived! But there is nothing to be revived in the unconverted. They don't need revival—they need resurrection!

I prefer to call this resurrection a 'great awakening'. If revival is for the church, that revival is ultimately to reach out to the lost for whom Christ died. What we need is for the eyes and ears of the lost to be opened to Christ and his offer of forgiveness and eternal life.

Revivals and great awakenings rarely come with dignified respectability.

Respectable or spiritual?

Roger Forster, with his academic and theologically sophisticated training, has commented: 'A respectable church will never turn a nation round to God.' Is the work of the Holy Spirit restricted because he is working in sophisticated churches? Are we living in an age where it is acceptable to be enthusiastic about football, rugby, cricket and tennis, or steam trains and films, or interior decoration and fashion—but if you are enthusiastic about your faith, suspicion emerges regarding your mental state?

'He is an enthusiastic young man' was often said of

me in the 70s and 80s in a half-honourable, half-dismissive fashion. One Christian minister came to see me recently to speak about the 'terrible dangers of enthusiasm'. Coming from his background I wanted to talk about the 'terrible dangers of cerebral theology'. From personal experience I have often found that those who feel they are sent to deliver the church from enthusiasm and the emotional are often the most enthusiastic and hopelessly over-emotional about their own perspectives! But *their* emotionalism is apparently conviction.

An untidy conclusion

The reason I have spent a considerable amount of time unpacking the issue of Pharisaism is because the great awakening that is taking place throughout the world will draw hostile fire from those who claim to be true Evangelicals, defenders of orthodoxy or theologically trained. Under such a barrage, I prophesy that many will cave in, deny their experience of the Holy Spirit or reduce it to emotionalism and will end up as dead and ineffective as they were before they hungered after the baptism in the Holy Spirit.

Jonathan Edwards only lived for fifty-five years. He has been called the greatest philosopher/theologian yet to grace the American scene. By the age of thirteen years he had a working knowledge of Latin, Greek and Hebrew, and was even writing papers on philosophy! He attended Yale in 1716 at the age of thirteen years. What is known as the Great Awakening took place between 1734 and 1735 and the more extensive revival in 1740–41 when he became a firm friend of George Whitefield. They travelled throughout America preaching in the open air, and church buildings that could barely contain the crowds. Paul Helm noted: 'In Edwards, as in Augustine, there is a union of highly intellectual and speculative spirit and an often ecstatic devotion to God in Christ.' He continued, 'Edwards was a complete stranger to that separation of heart and head that has often plagued evangelical religion.'

Edwards and his colleagues saw tens of thousands come to Christ. But he saw not only genuine conversions but spurious ones as well. He witnessed first hand ecstatic phenomena that could be directly attributed to the Holy Spirit *and* to various abuses. But he saw that God could have a purpose in bringing error to light at the start of a spiritual awakening:

> If God intends this great revival of religion to be dawning, or a forerunner of an happy state of His church on earth, it may be an instance of the divine wisdom, in the beginning of it, to supplant so many irregularities and errors in combat, to which He knew men, in their present weak state, were most exposed, under great religious affections and when animated with great zeal. For it will be very likely to be of excellent benefit to His church, in the continuance and progress of the work afterwards: their experience in the first setting out of the mischievous consequences of these errors, and smarting for them in the beginning, may be an happy defence to them afterwards, for many generations, from these errors which otherwise they might continually be exposed to.
>
> (Jonathan Edwards, *Some Thoughts*)

Modern-day Pharisees see themselves as defenders of the faith, and in so doing resist and oppose the Holy Spirit and those exercising the gifts of the Spirit.

But here is the rub. Words spoken against Christ can be forgiven—what grace! But words spoken against the Holy Spirit cannot be forgiven either 'in this age' or in the 'age to come' (Mt 12:32). In other words, proclaiming that the results of Holy Spirit activity are at best lies and deception, and at worst demonic, is in fact unforgivable. Read it how you wish, but that is what it says.

A vision may fill one's soul and a mission one's daily life, and even though the price is being paid and the church subsequently being shaped, opposition from the so-called Christian community will nearly always be the first thing that hits when a great awakening or revival begins to emerge.

The pharisaical mindset will always be suspicious of anything that involves emotions. Pharisees control their own emotions with vigorous attention to detail. And yet the Great Awakening that took place in America in 1740 was often characterised by states of ecstasy and convulsions. It was true of the remarkable revival in Azusa Street on the west coast of America, and of the Welsh revival that took place at a similar time. And contrary to what some may think, the Welsh revival was taking place quite independently of what was happening in America—indeed, Americans sent a deputation over to the Welsh revival to find out what was happening.

Old time religion?

Mr Lindsay Clegg was a leading Evangelical in Britain throughout the 1940s, 50s and 60s. One of the many initiatives he started was the Filey Week, with a strong emphasis on teaching and mission. Until of late it was suspicious and even hostile to the charismatic movement, and some participants still are.

Lindsay told me how he was converted in the Welsh revival. He went on to explain that a man seated by him had fallen across his lap in an emotional state. Lindsay was embarrassed and troubled, but through it found the Saviour. 'It was so emotional—but so real,' he observed.

So what can we conclude?

1. Revival is for the church—we need to be revived in faith and in the power of the Holy Spirit. A great awakening is for the lost, when they become aware that God is in the land and salvation is possible.

2. Both great awakenings and revivals are untidy. The Spirit of God graciously blows and speaks alongside human frailty, sin, denominational tradition and even demonic activity. After all, the church in Corinth was in a state of disorder at the same time as being most active in the gifts of the Spirit.

3. The Holy Spirit does not lift off when the theologically trained would like him to. The Spirit stirs emotions to purify faith, belief and experience, whereas Pharisees want to stop anything they consider unorthodox and emotional and from their point of view untraditional.

4. It is often the biblically committed who are devoid of an outward experience of the Holy Spirit, who will oppose revival or a great awakening as much, if not more, than the unbeliever.

Match point

Any lingering belief in the supernatural was strongly erased by David Hume, an English philosopher who died in 1776. Observing a church which did not believe in the miraculous, he concluded that since no miracles are evident in the here and now, none ever took place in the early church. In other words, the Bible is full of romantic fairy tales at best, or lies at worst.

Yet those lies and fantasies took Paul through prison, beatings, torture, hunger, betrayal and, if history is correct, eventual beheading. And all of this for a vision on the road to Damascus and a new interpretation of the Scriptures.

Over that same period of time thousands of mums and dads, single adults and teenagers were tarred at Nero's garden parties and set on fire for entertainment. They were killed by gladiators, ripped apart by lions in arenas or simply died in prison after many years. The original disciples were all martyred for their faith (except for John, exiled on Patmos), and not one of them is recorded as recanting, owning up to fantastic stories or inventions.

Not only were they interpreting Scripture differently, but their outward manifestations, experiences and tangible evidences of the sick being healed, the demonised being delivered and lives being changed through this gospel, convinced them of their deep convictions.

But pre-eminently, for those early disciples and thousands more who followed from afar, there was this Christ—this charismatic teacher who was morally upright, kind and gracious, but had continual run-ins with the religious authorities, who claimed to be the guardians of tradition and the upholders of scriptural teachings.

'Other sheep'

Recently, I lunched with the Archdeacon of an Anglican diocese, a man who would not be keen to call himself evangelical. Talking of answers to prayer he told me, 'Early on in my marriage many things had happened which discouraged me. It seemed to be one thing after another, as often happens. We had no money. I was under a lot of pressure and most unhappy. Then one day, the exhaust went on my car. It was the last straw. I had had enough. I eventually got home and said to my wife, "If I was an Evangelical, I would pray, put my trust in God, and a miracle would happen and an envelope would drop through the door with money in it to pay the bill for my exhaust." Before I could go any further she interrupted, "Well, you'd better sit down, because that is exactly what has happened. While you were out, somebody put this envelope through the door." It was more than sufficient to pay for the bill. I was humbled and mystified.'

'Why mystified?' I enquired. He then explained that he believed in miracles, he had experienced them himself and had heard firsthand stories from people he trusted, who had not put themselves in the evangelical or charismatic mould. But then he asked, 'Why should God care about my exhaust when there is so much hunger in Africa, the slaughter of innocents in Europe and massive social problems including child abuse, theft and racism in America and other parts of the world?'

Rightly or wrongly, I did not feel this was the time to give him the depth of my wisdom, theological insights or quick and easy answers. Here was a man acknowledging the subjective and mysterious activity of the Holy Spirit. 'It cannot be denied,' he said. And yet he had many questions about a world of suffering and a God, who, to the best of his knowledge, seemed either without power or concern for people who had never seen a car, never mind had their exhaust drop off.

I could have helped him by talking about nations which have hounded Christians out, imprisoned Christian leaders and where the name of Christ is now unknown. One is hardly likely to expect a spiritual and godly revival to take place in such a situation, and as nature abhors a vacuum, demons rush in and dark forces take over. Or I could have spoken about the 'moment' which is all life consists of. After the resurrection we shall look back on our 'light momentary affliction', as the Apostle Paul calls it, and realise that our destiny depended on what we did with our moment.

And, surely, the God of all grace and mercy will do what is right to those who have never heard, who lived through starvation, death, abuse and torture. He can be trusted.

Because of the Archdeacon's humility, he bowed to the sovereignty of the work of the Holy Spirit, but also to the mysteries about life and death, suffering and abuse. He almost expressed a 'groan which cannot be uttered'. It was to him a complete mystery—an embarrassment, even—why God would make provision for his transport while other greater needs seemed to be unattended.

It is not difficult to admire such humility and questions when a man then puts his faith in the living God alongside the unanswered questions.

Twins in the womb?

Jesus' best friend John said that he was 'full of grace and truth'. The order in which things are written in the Scriptures is often important. Grace came before truth!

As Christians, many of us are full of grace, but not so strong on truth, and barely know one end of our Bible from the other. This will lead to mixture—a blurring of our message—and we will be lost in a sea of sentimentality, likes and dislikes, and a view of Christ which is unconnected to Scripture. The willingness of some to identify and work with any who simply call themselves

Christians, irrespective of what they believe and how they live, is a symptom of this. It is more New Age than biblical; more the spirit of the age than the Spirit of Christ.

Others of us are very strong on truth. Truth matters. Jesus said, 'I am the truth.' It has been said that the Bible is the intelligence of the Holy Spirit. An inadequate description maybe, but Scripture has been preserved for us at a colossal price (as we have just read) in order that we may know the truth and the truth that makes up the body of doctrine we call 'the faith'.

An understanding of grace will create humility—that God in his mercy should have anything to do with us in the first place. But a knowledge of Scripture will also give us a love for the truth which creates clarity.

Without grace we become harsh with our clarity. Without truth we become soft on theology and the message we have been given. The gospel is reduced to the fact that God loves us and he accepts us as we are. But as it has been said so often before, he loves us too much to leave us the way we are!

Grace and truth, humility and clarity. I have been an observer of several inter-church leadership events where humility was thick on the ground and a willingness to listen to each other evident. But they couldn't give you the correct time, never mind correct theology! Then I have been in other situations where truth has been taught with such clarity that any hint of believing other than what was the given subscribed theology would cause you to be marginalised immediately.

The temptation to keep control

Leadership doesn't want to upset the flock. Everything is controlled. Control is a massive problem in most churches.

The Apostle Paul had laid the foundation and given direction to the massive church in Corinth. Several thousand people were doing a lot of things right. But baptism for the dead? Grabbing food and leaving others hungry at the Lord's table? Tongues without interpretations? Self-indulgence with charismata? There was even a question about whether they believed the resurrection. His corrective letter tells them how to put things in order, and avoid going to excess; how to deal with 'the world, the flesh and the devil'. But he goes on to encourage relationships, love, intimacy and, believe it or not, the gifts of the Holy Spirit.

To his churches across Galatia (not a town but a wide area like a county or state) he tells them they have been 'bewitched'. Strong language. Verging on the occult. Why? Because they were into control. This is always a human answer—the decent and respectable thing to do when things are out of order. People want control because they believe they have the truth.

Truth and experience

So how do we know the truth?

Cramming our brains with knowledge is not always wrong. There is no virtue in an empty head. But accumulating statistics and data regarding biblical history, geography and personalities, as well as doctrine, is more a Western phenomenon than a scriptural idea.

Hungry after the truth, knowing the truth and communicating the truth are certainly bound up with remembering and recalling facts and figures and biblical ideas, and if all these things are done to develop our relationship with Christ and to be refilled with his Spirit on a daily basis, all well and good. But the keen Bible reader, book reviewer, concordance lover and learner of Greek and Hebrew could be in for a subtle shift of emphasis and purpose.

In the Scriptures there is harmony between knowing and knowledge. On a late night chat show you may hear rock star, actor or actress say, 'Yes of course I knew him, but not in a biblical way of course!' This is normally followed by a brief spell of laughter. When Scripture says that Adam 'knew' Eve, it doesn't mean he 'knew' what she had for supper, what clothes she liked and that she had a weakness for forbidden fruit. Knowing somebody in biblical terms implied relationship, love and responsibility.

When as a teenager I sat in a Gospel Hall—a small Plymouth Brethren Assembly twenty miles south west of London—I was often confused. I sat looking at a Bible text painted onto the wall in gold leaf. It confused me for years. It was simple enough: 'I am the way, the truth and the life.'

How on earth can a person be the way? Surely they can only point the way? How can a person be the truth? You can tell the truth, write the truth and verbally communicate the truth, but how can you *be* the truth? The last bit didn't worry me. Jesus had life, and as Creator and Redeemer he was the originator and the sustainer of life. But this truth business bothered me. How can truth be a personality as against an understanding of accurate data? But the Bible is very specific. Jesus is the truth. We are invited to know the truth—and enter into relationship.

The only things we know about God are those things he has chosen to reveal about himself to us. I do not know anything about God, and nor do you, other than what he has chosen to reveal to us through creation, law, prophets, the rest of Scripture and Christ himself. We should never forget: God is under no obligation to reveal anything of himself to us in any way whatever.

Truth is about persons, and what they do. Endeavouring to reflect the true meaning of biblical Greek, Roger Forster often talks about Jesus 'kinging it' or Christians 'truthing it'.

Samuel Taylor-Coleridge called Paul's letter to the Ephesian believers the 'divinest literature on earth'. Writing from prison he urges the believers to grow up 'speaking the truth in love'. And then he goes on to talk about the body of Christ growing up together so that it 'builds itself up in love, as each part does its work' (Eph 4:15–16). 'Speaking the truth in love' is literally 'truthing it'. So just as 'knowing' someone in biblical language goes way beyond reading their biography or listening to gossip, and speaks of intimacy, trust and relationships, so 'knowing the truth' is more than reading facts and figures and living by them (modern-day Pharisaism). It entails intimacy, a relationship with Christ; with a God who speaks today, not one who spoke once then left us a book to live by. And this sort of Christianity—authentic Christianity, New Testament Christianity—will throw into sharp contrast a Christianity which is mental agreement, statements (albeit biblical statements) and a non-relational approach to church.

I suggest, therefore, that all biblical theology has been worked out in the crucible of experience. And I would go further and say that the prophetic Scriptures were only understood after the event, and sometimes decades after. It took a quick witted, anointed and bold Peter to say, 'This is that.' Though much of 'that' did not happen on the Day of Pentecost and hasn't happened since. But he was speaking the truth. He *knew* this was the Holy Spirit—prophesied, predicted and now experienced. The crucial crux of good theology is the direct link between Scripture and an ongoing spiritual experience. Separate them and you have modern-day Pharisaism or Gnosticism.

New Testament Christianity saw discipleship in terms of forgiving sinners, healing the sick, casting out demons and a life of sacrifice. It is obvious that knowledge of the Scriptures came into that. 'Study to show yourself approved,' Paul wrote to Timothy. But this is not the primary mark of discipleship, for if it were the Pharisees would not have had their ears boxed verbally by Christ on so many occasions.

The harvest

One thing we can be sure of: whatever we sow, we reap.

What we are currently reaping is in direct relationship to what we have sown in years past. Many Christians are in quiet rebellion against Scripture, or against the Holy Spirit, or both. Look at the fruit. Yet from a scriptural point of view, obedience is normal and disobedience is abnormal.

There is an interesting fact about reaping contained in A.T. Pierson's book *The Bible and Spiritual Life*. Over 400 descendants have been traced of Jonathan Edwards (born in 1703, born again in 1721), the leader of the Great Awakening in the USA. He himself was one of eleven children, and was the only son among ten sisters! Of those descendants the following have been traced:

    2 Vice presidents
    6 Congressmen
  14 University presidents
100 Professors
100 Preachers of the gospel and missionaries
120 Lawyers and judges
  60 Doctors

It has been said that almost every major American industry has had a descendant of Jonathan Edwards involved in it—and he died when he was fifty-five years of age.

Contrast that with the family of Abraham Jakes—a man who turned his back on the grace of God. More than 1,200 of his descendants have been traced, and this is what they found:

  400 Alcoholics and drug addicts
  810 Beggars
  130 Convicted criminals
   80 Habitual thieves and pick-pockets
    7 Murderers, hanged or executed on the electric chair

Out of that vast number, only twenty ever learned a trade—and most of those in prison!

Radical disciples are likely to produce radical disciples.

God is extremely gracious. While honouring him and his word in one area, we can resist him in another. Those who resist God may also resist us! However, we must never fight fire with fire. Many people may not be our enemies, but do act like our enemies. We are told to love our enemies. As we deal with opposition from within our own ranks, we must understand that the tools of our warfare are not guns and bullets, baseball bats and flick knives. We are called to love where there is prejudice; to extend grace when there is legalistic clarity; to pray for people who don't care for us; to choose to serve when others choose to control. Our invitation to relationship with Christ is an invitation to love those around us.

True spirituality is not learned among the friends we have chosen. God's love is best discovered and expressed where we cannot be selective.

Marshall Shelley once wrote: 'The family and the church are not joined by invitation only. We have no choice about who our parents or brothers and sisters will be; yet we are expected to love them. Neither can we choose who will or will not be in the family of God; any who confess Jesus as Lord must be welcome.'

Shelley tells the story of Tachomius, an Egyptian soldier converted to Christ by the kindness of Christians in Thebes. When he was released from the military, he was baptised. This was around AD 315. He became a disciple of Palamon, an ascetic who led him into self-denial and the lonely life of a hermit. Sadly, in first-century Christianity, quite often the model of devotion was opting out of culture, wandering the desert, fasting, praying and having ecstatic spiritual experiences. Some ate nothing but grass, lived in trees and refused to wash. This was so often the accepted image of holiness. It spoke of being alone, being silent and being severe. But then Tachomius began to question his faith environment. How can you learn to love, extend kindness or be patient when no one else is around?

We are often surrounded by disagreeable people who claim to know Christ better than we do. We are called at times to say some hard things to one another and to 'truth it'. But we are never called to resentment, superiority or arrogance—even quiet arrogance. If we are not satisfied with our own spiritual lives (and I trust we are not), there is no need to behave in a self-satisfied way with others—even those who oppose us.

In an age when the spiritual journey seems more important than what a person believes, we must focus on love *and* truth, and allow the dynamic experience of the Holy Spirit to do some unusual things. We will face opposition, but every revival has faced opposition and every great awakening has as well. Let's face it, much will come from Pharisees. We must love them, but also speak the truth in love. That's what Jesus did.

Learning how to handle opposition affects the quality of our work and more importantly our relationships. It will also help us shape our future. But the future will be determined by what we do now—in the present.

So what now?

6

Living in the Present

Do you think that it was self-denial for the Lord Jesus to come down from heaven to rescue the world? No. It was love—love that swallows up everything, and first of all self.
                    Ludwig Von Zinzendorf to John Wesley

Christianity is on a new path, gathering momentum as millions join the journey with a purpose.

Whenever there has been a revival or great awakening, it has always been because Jesus Christ as a person has emerged as a living hope, a vibrant reality, and has brought light to the darkness of individuals and entire communities.

So how can we plan to be here for the 'long haul', as Tom Marshall calls it, or invest into the next generation? Why is that important? Because some from every generation of Christians who have ever lived thought Jesus would come back in their own generation, and he has not! If we do not learn from that, the revival and awakening will be localised and short-lived. Instead of success, we shall experience failure.

Having been involved in evangelism, church planting and social action on a local and national level for some twenty-five years, there are a number of things I have learned about failure and success. I have also learned so much from others who have modelled their faith and the practice of that faith in ways that have encouraged me to keep on, when from a natural point of view I would have levelled off, and perhaps even given up.

Let's be practical

How can we hasten the Lord's coming (2 Pet 3:12)? How can we ensure as much as possible that we are around for the long haul, remaining effective and fruitful despite blurred vision, a slow pace of mission and subtle opposition?

The present, and the choices we make, will determine our future.

I know of many Christians who have been hurt, or lost their way, and have ended up out of Christian friendship, now 'free' to believe and serve the Lord. What they mean is that they are free not to worship with others; they are free not to give towards the Lord's work; they are free not to pray together; they are free not to share their faith in specific ways and they are free not to invite anybody to anything to expose them to God's love. Their freedom can only be equated with an ocean liner lying on a dry bed. Such a ship is truly free—free of the sea. But ships are made for the sea, as we are made for Christian fellowship and friendship, corporate worship and prayer, and the sharing of our faith, identifying in words and deeds with the powerless and the marginalised.

In these situations, those who have been hurt and disillusioned need a change of heart, mind and direction (biblical repentance). Repentance is not simply feeling sorry for the position one is in. Repentance is a change of direction.

C.S. Lewis made it clear that repentance is not what we have to do before God will have us back; it is simply a description of the route back!

Past present?

Decisions we have made in the past that have been biblical, helpful, healthy and hopeful are usually directly related to our present circumstances, relationships, finances, personal and general morality, and usefulness.

Equally, bad decisions that have been left unattended through pride or ignorance also affect where we are today. Many of those who are without jobs, sick in hospital, divorced, lonely or in prison or psychiatric hospitals are so as a direct result of decisions that have been made, which have remained without a change of heart, mind or direction. That is not to imply all illness, or even imprisonment, is due to wrongdoing. But there is a direct link in many situations between unhealthy living and ill health, imprisonment and wrong choices! However, where we have found grace to repent, change direction and make amends, that change of direction has again affected our circumstances and our attitude. If our present is largely determined by our past, it follows that the future will be much determined by the present.

If we are going to be here for the long haul instead of a short sprint, what are the lessons that will help us in success and failure?

I believe that one of the roles of those of us who travel is not to give endless 'messages'. Rather we should help people to understand what they have seen, heard and experienced in other situations, particularly where they have been able to adopt many of those observations which have improved the quality of their ministry and work. In some twenty-five years of travel, I have seen, learned and absorbed a number of things which have helped me in my own ministry. I offer them to you.

1. Build team

Without trust, progress is impossible. Whether we are working with youth or musicians, in pastoral work or evangelism, in social action or written communication, we need to work in team.

We should thank God for the mighty Christian super-stars such as Mother Teresa or Billy Graham, who have become mighty simply by serving God. They are often made mighty as a result of the media—Christian or otherwise. The Bible is full of such personalities, deliberately highlighted and drawn to our attention by the Holy Spirit. They existed in Bible days, both in the Old and New Testaments, and so not surprisingly exist today.

But God is a trinity, a team. His purposes are corporate and not merely individualistic. If we are going to build team we must build in a high trust factor, as all teams have found. Many groups have a low trust factor due to the way they treat each other in both success and failure.

So how do we create a high trust factor?

We love people, without any thought of return.
We are sensitive to the mistakes that others make.
We give, in a self-centred situation.
We honour our words and promises.

We think of and weigh other perspectives than our own.

We deny ourselves luxurious self-indulgent idiosyncrasies.

We are unafraid to ask for help even from those junior to ourselves.

We acknowledge our weaknesses as well as our strengths.

We pray that others will do better than we have done.

We believe in people, expressing God's belief in them.

This creates trust, whether one is working with a fixed team or in a general team of responsible people.

Knowing our strengths is vital, but knowing our weaknesses is often even more vital if we are going to create team.

Heaven is a team. Adam became team. We see team throughout the Old Testament of prophets and judges, priests and leaders. Jesus did the same after he had been baptised—he called for a team and built into them a high trust factor.

No person is better than their team. I would say to all those who are leading and those who desire to lead:

If we expect love we must give love.

If we expect care we must offer care.

If we expect mercy we must show mercy.

If we expect forgiveness we must extend forgiveness.

That builds trust, which builds team, which reflects heaven.

2. Eradicate professionalism

To be effective and professional is admirable. There is no virtue in being ineffective and amateurish. There is no premium on good intentions. They are inadequate to fulfil Christ's mission. It is important we learn from others. We should also be selective in our priorities—we cannot do everything at once!

But there is a professionalism which is more concerned about image than reality; about the organisation and ministry rather than people.

The first-century disciples endeavoured to be effective. Somebody has said, 'If we believed what they believed, maybe we might achieve what they achieved!' Seeking to be effective and professional in one's writing, public oratory, counselling, musical skills, biblical studies and administration is to be commended. But professionalism as an 'ism' is solely concerned with pleasing the board and ourselves. Professionalism in this sense takes place when we become quite detached from the people we are serving. I know not a few who are publicly excellent, even brilliant, in style and content—but privately? That is another story.

I often remember the words of a leading international figure who, while walking with me in his city, asked concerning a friend of mine, 'Why is it he can appear to be so opinionated and hostile on the platform when he is such a nice person in real life?' I was not quite sure what he was getting at, so I replied, 'Why do you ask that?' He replied, 'Because most Christian leaders we know are very nice on the platform, but not so nice in private life!' I realised this was a compliment for my friend!

A mild dose of spiritual schizophrenia is always attached to professionalism. You can actually get to a place where the two lives are so separate that one is barely on a nodding acquaintance with the other.

Professionalism is always the first step towards religiosity. One does not need to dress up in clerical garb to be religious. There are many who do that who are not at all religious. But there are others who wear quite normal attire who are religious from a pentecostal or charismatic point of view—a front for other things.

We must acknowledge that there is no direct link we can find in Scripture between how we operate publicly and true spirituality. There are many who operate very well from a public point of view on platforms and in the media, whose private lives nevertheless are out of order.

Confession of sin and failure helps eradicate professionalism. Confession brings things out into the light. The light does not change a thing; it simply reveals the thing for what it is.

3. Refuse to live without confrontation

What we refuse to confront has a habit of turning around and smacking us in the face some months later.

There are a few who feel it their God-given mandate to confront, challenge and question, provoking and annoying anyone they can. It comes from a spirit so unlike that of our Lord, who only said the hard things when he had to, and then with apparent sadness and reluctance.

The majority of us, however, never confront. At best we simply 'pray about it'.

Joshua was like that. He was told to confront the people of Israel with their wrongdoing, but instead he decided to fast and pray—accompanied by ashes and horsehair for good measure. But the Lord told him, in as many words, that there are times when it is wrong to pray, and the only way forward is to confront (Josh 7:10–13). Leaders—true leaders—must be willing to confront.

I have often been surprised at people who have been dishonest with their tax returns, those who have been sleeping with their boyfriend or girlfriend, or who have gossiped and even told outright lies in the full knowledge that other people know. But those 'other people' are not confrontational. Those involved in such unbiblical behaviour know they will never be confronted, challenged or gently redirected. Cowardice caused eyes to be diverted, ears to be blocked and unfaithfulness to be overlooked. Almost all of these situations lead to tragedy.

If we are to find favour in the eyes of God, we must ask him to put sinews of steel in our souls. Then with his grace and mercy we must be willing to confront friends and partners, to win rather than isolate, to bless rather than curse, to help them choose rightly both for the present and the future. Right choices bring peace.

Peace is not an absence of conflict. It is being in the presence of God, knowing that we are doing his will and pleasing him. All of this is clear in the light of Scripture and is not open to private interpretation and feelings. God deliver us from non-confrontational lifestyles.

Our Lord allows us to get away with things we are not meant to allow one another to get away with. The New Testament is full of evidence, teaching us that we have a responsibility to be the eyes and ears, as well as the heart and mind, of Christ. But confrontation doesn't mean sitting eye-ball to eye-ball, wagging our index finger at people. Those found with sin in their lives and those who find themselves out of order with Scripture often want change or a way of escape. The Holy

Spirit may have been resisted and Scripture may have been rejected, but when individuals are sitting with the results of that resistance and disobedience they are often desperate for a way out. Guilt and shame pile in to make a proper response difficult. In an ideal world repentance, confession and apology should be expected. But life is never as ideal as we would like it to be. So a gentle, forgiving arm around someone, with a helpful 'What can I do to help you in this situation?' is, I suggest, a hundred times more effective than a raised, angry, confrontational voice. We have to ask ourselves when dealing with issues and when confronting people, whether we want to win them or simply point out their error.

4. Watch the company you keep!

It is true—you *can* tell a person by the company they keep. You can also tell a company by the individuals it keeps!

We are all called to love the lost, disillusioned and cynical. But as much as possible it should be a one-way traffic! As men and women of faith, we are called to influence the hurt and disillusioned, the cynical and pessimistic. We do not want to be unduly influenced by them. They may have things to say which we need to hear, but we do not want them imparting their spirit and attitudes to us.

It is interesting to note that King David's wife Michal is not once referred to as 'Michal, David's wife'. She is always referred to as 'Saul's daughter'. She was never known as the wife of a man of God, but the daughter of a demonised man who failed. How will you be known?

Will you be one who identified with men and women

of God (aware of their failures), or one identified with the cynical and disillusioned, the isolated and individualistic, those who can comment on everything and are committed to nothing?

Moses led the Israelites out of Egypt. Depending which commentator you read, there were probably between one and two million of them at least. They had visions of the promised land, but only two made it. Why? They stopped believing and they started complaining.

Complaining is easy, contagious, damaging and faith-destroying. You cannot believe and complain at the same time. Complaining creates a darkness of the soul. God promised 'milk and honey' to Moses and the Children of Israel, but they were then led into a desert where at times there was not even any water! When great promises have been made to a life or a church, God nearly always takes us through a desert experience. Then it is either a time for faith or another round of complaining.

All leaders fail at times. King David failed. Moses failed. The Apostle Paul failed.

All leaders make mistakes. A certain Captain Edward Smith had never made a maritime error. That is why he was chosen to take charge of the maiden voyage of the Titanic!

People who have never made mistakes are the most dangerous people in the church. Not that people who have not made mistakes exist, of course. They only pretend they have not made mistakes. Or they might even believe they have never made any mistakes. That is why we must produce churches which allow people to sin. You might be shocked by that, but the alternative is that we produce churches which do not allow people to sin. So what do they do when they do sin? They have to cover it up, hide it and pretend. We should create churches which allow people to sin, so that when people come to a place of confession and repentance, we, as friends, colleagues and leaders, are not continually shocked and will be able to help.

The things we hide dominate us. As we endeavour to become closer and more productive disciples of Christ, we need to be continually finding faith, walking in it and dealing with a complaining tongue and its complaining company.

It is easy to live in the past—to want today to be much as it was yesterday, yesteryear, yesterdecade. I have often heard people saying, as they are about to leave a church, 'This is not the church I joined!' Thank God for that! I am glad that Pioneer People, the church I lead, is not the same today as it was in 1980. It is not the same church it was in 1990 and I pray that by the year 2000 it will have grown beyond recognition. Many who have been in the church a long time will, I hope, be taking up further responsibilities of pastoral care, prayer, evangelism and social action.

We are in great danger of producing perennial infants. This comes about when we have the overwhelming minority ministering to the overwhelming majority who feel they have a right to be cared for, loved, pampered and generally attended to. As we have seen, the whole role of pastoral ministry is to teach people to take responsibility for themselves and then for others—this is maturity. We should be planning for growth instead of complaining *when* we grow or when our roles change.

Let us encourage each other to count our blessings and 'name them one by one'; to be a resource for one another rather than a dumping ground for one another's verbal rubbish.

In an age of uncertainty it becomes easy to retreat to safe areas. We sometimes need to ask ourselves when we last took a chance. Sin and insecurity intimidate us and we can use them to intimidate others, particularly those who want to move on, move up and move out. We end up complaining, and resisting the very people who can lead us out of our current malaise.

5. Do not devalue tradition

Tradition in and of itself is neither good nor bad. For to be sure, we all know there are bad traditions, but we need to remember there are some good ones as well.

We have all sat around someone else's meal table waiting in embarrassed silence for 'grace'. By the time it comes the meal is half cold, and we are just going through a traditional routine. (I often think it would be better to give thanks for a meal after the food has been eaten, as that would have a lot more integrity and reality to it.)

Few of us have not been subjected to meaningless tradition in church. We preach the gospel on a Sunday evening to the converted. But you cannot change it—it is the gospel meeting, always has been, always will be. We take bread and wine (or a wafer and grape juice as often happens) without even talking to each other. We may be 'communing' with God, but not to one another. Is this another unbiblical tradition? But suggest we talk to each other, put our arms round each other and share bread and wine together, and many churches would have a corporate heart attack.

Hundreds and hundreds of churches still go out

knocking on doors to put a few more people off! 'Well at least they heard,' somebody said to me when I asked them why they were not more creative in reaching their community.

Not only have we all experienced meaningless tradition, bad tradition and fruitless tradition—most of us have been damaged by it as well. To challenge it is costly; to come out of it is sacrificial.

But there are good traditions. We need to embrace certain traditions—the ones I call 'familiar landmarks', signposts along the way—because they point us to better things.

The tradition of extending the right hand of friendship or embracing is a good one, and infinitely better than what often amounts to hardly an acknowledgement.

Joining hands to thank God for a meal (before or after!) is infinitely better than 'saying grace' as some sort of religious exercise. Being thankful for food and drink, particularly with guests, is important, but that doesn't mean we slavishly have to do it every time we eat a hamburger, have morning cornflakes or grill cheese on toast late at night.

Inviting people into our homes to eat and drink, both believers and unbelievers, is another good tradition. Entire churches are noted for their hospitality or lack of it. And I, perhaps more than most readers, have suffered and been blessed at the hands of both categories. With the latter, one always wants to apologise for upsetting their normal routine, while the others make you feel at home immediately.

The tradition of giving financially to God, to his work and to needs is one that reflects the giving heart of God. What did God do for a getting, grabbing, power-hungry world? He 'gave his only Son'. He broke into the cycle of attaining, acquiring and hoarding by giving someone away. Giving is a good tradition.

Whenever we have a speaker at Pioneer People or in one of our national Pioneer Leadership Conferences, we talk about what we are going to give the speaker beforehand, irrespective of whether he or she performs well or not. 'The servant is worthy of his or her hire.' As we talk we have a sense of what is appropriate, and if it is in the local church I will often say to Nigel Day, 'Well, what are we going to give? This or that?' He will always say, reflecting my own heart, and more importantly that of the heart of God, 'Let's err on the side of generosity.' God is not an economist—creation itself reveals that. He is a generous, giving God.

We communicate at different levels. Late one summer I spoke at a series of meetings in Bristol with David Day and his church. When I arrived in my room there were two or three bunches of fresh flowers, probably taken from the garden. There was a bowl of sweets, a bottle of sherry for my wife (who was unable to join me for that weekend) and a card with a kind warm message written in it. Having had a very full day and evening, I awoke on Sunday morning to find fresh coffee and a newspaper for me. They had even found out if I wanted breakfast and what newspaper I read. I read *The Independent on Sunday* (it is OK to take Sunday papers—it is Monday papers you shouldn't take as they are printed on a Sunday!).

All of this communicated something. It probably cost no more than £5 for all of that, but a cheque ten times that amount couldn't make up for the comfort, friendship and warmth I felt, which gave me such a good platform from which to speak.

I have spoken in a previous chapter about the 'traditions of the elders' which have more to do with the Talmud than the Torah. These traditions were unbendable and merciless. But as we discern between fixed morality and ethics and flexible traditions, we will be enabled to gauge our growth and effectiveness.

6. Stay in faith and prayer

Some scientists tell us that what we see with our eyes finalises all discussion about the structure of matter. Scripture, however, tells us differently. Faith, or faithful prayer, can not only affect the seen, but can look into the unseen. Faith not only finalises matters but actually changes matters and events. 'Faith is the assurance of things hoped for, the conviction of things not seen' (Heb 11:1, RSV).

Talking to God about individuals, people groups and situations changes the way we talk to those people and view those situations.

However, there are still many Christians who are cessationists—that is, they believe that certain gifts of the Holy Spirit ceased when the canon of Scripture was finalised. They can only pray, 'Your will be done,' as healing isn't the norm, and answered prayers have little to do with their faith, more the sovereignty of God. I would like to point out, however, that when Peter walked on the water, this was not to do with the sovereignty of God, but Peter's faith. When it failed—he sank!

Cessationists may pray for healing, but not in faith. They do not expect God to speak to them: they have the Bible. But this cessationist view has been overtaken by individuals, churches and entire nations hurrying after a more dynamic experience of God. In addition, a great deal of scholarship and theological study has shown how hollow and desolate the cessationist view is.

Counterfeit prophecy and miracles there may be, but wherever there is a counterfeit it follows that there must be the original! Why counterfeit the gifts of the Holy Spirit if there are no more originals around today?

Given or taken

A story is told that when Paul Getty died, his accountant was asked, 'What did he leave?' Without a pause the accountant replied, 'Everything—absolutely everything!'

When Christ left the earth to take his throne in heaven, Scripture leads us to believe that he left his church 'everything, absolutely everything'.

C.I. Schofield accepted a cessationist or dispensational view of Scripture. This affected both the USA and Europe. The 1907 original version of Schofield's Bible notes that the church at Corinth was swept towards a 'childish delight in sign gifts, rather than sober instruction'. John Calvin, A.N. Groves, John Darby and B.B. Warfield all fell under the spell of rationalism. Prayer and faith were general rather than specific. Faith became 'the faith'—something quite different.

To stay in faith and prayer, you need to put yourself around men and women of faith and prayer. Prayer produces spiritual health. That is the blessed state where we can enjoy our God in high praises and adoration, along with others. But it is also the place where we feel the heart of God for a heartless, oppressive and desperate world.

In a recent survey taken in the USA, 74% of Christians are thinking 'a lot more' about spiritual warfare. Prayer is becoming more meaningful as evil takes hold. Spiritual warfare is all about strongholds. What is a stronghold? Anything that has a strong hold on you, or on a people group, a church, a town or a nation.

Biblical prayer and faith do several things:

(a) Prayer creates a climate for clarity and wisdom

This relates to the home as well as the work place; to church as well as leisure time. It is relevant as we share our faith with the not-yet Christians around us. 'Do not be anxious about anything, but in everything, by prayer and petition, with thanksgiving, present your requests to God. And the peace of God, which transcends all understanding, will guard your hearts and your minds in Christ Jesus' (Phil 4:6–7). Prayer brings things out into the light and gives clarity, as all light does.

(b) Prayer increases anointing and favour

Nehemiah explains, when he needed help, 'I prayed to the God of heaven, and I answered the king, "If it pleases the king and if your servant has found favour in his sight, let him send me"' (Neh 2:4–6). It has been said that the church is only the church when it is responding to God. When it is not, it is simply going through a religious routine. Perhaps a Christian is only a Christian when he or she is responding to Christ. Prayer is a major part of that response. A praying people find favour with God.

(c) Prayer creates opportunity

Satan hinders prayers, quite simply because he wants the doors closed to us. He wants the gospel blocked. Satan wanted Peter, but Christ said that he had prayed for him. What would have happened if Christ had not prayed for him? Prayer creates an opportunity for us to love one another, care for one another and guard one another's backs instead of exposing each other, griping, complaining and judging people by our own standards. Prayer, it seems, is a major means of releasing divine power to frustrate Satan. Prayer opens doors.

It has been said, 'When we work, we work. When we pray, God works!'

(d) Prayer gives life meaning and purpose

One leading atheist once commented, 'My life has no meaning. I do not see why anyone else's life should have any meaning.' Bertrand Russell, another leading atheist halfway through this century, commented somewhat sadly, 'I know that to love is better than to hate—but I cannot tell you why.' It is clear that both of these atheists were not men of faith and prayer! Faith and prayer form a love relationship, and love is not a feeling but a series of choices. Thank God for feelings, but prayer and faith are matters of choice. Whether we pray while walking along kicking leaves, or speak to God in our home early in the morning, before dawn has barely broken, prayer and faith give us a perspective on life that nothing else can do. Stay in faith and prayer.

7. Read and apply Scripture

We cannot apply Scripture unless we have read it. Having read it, we must as individuals and groups apply the truth to all areas of our behaviour and strategy. I am often astounded at so-called mature Christians who say and do things that are diametrically opposed to Scripture and yet feel they have the right to do so!

In 1986 there were two electrical engineers in Chernobyl's nuclear plant who were performing what was later described as an 'unauthorised experiment'. So what were they doing? They were trying to discover how long a turbine would free wheel when they took the power off it. Reactors, it seems, are most unstable in their lower ranges. To perform their experiment, they had to manually override six separate computer-driven alarm systems! They ignored every single one. The result was reckoned to be the largest industrial accident in the world.

They overrode instructions created for their own safety, simply in order to experiment. Many Christians experiment with the truth or play around with Scripture. Scriptural truth can be accepted or rejected, but one thing it cannot be is changed!

Scripture gives us models for interpersonal relationships. It tells us how to behave towards enemies and those who act like enemies. The Bible gives us models of church for interpersonal discipline as well as for communicating the gospel in deed and word. One hundred years ago C.H. Spurgeon warned the church that it was drifting away from the point of a biblical gospel. And this is often done by those who know Scripture but don't apply it.

Truth must be a passion, not a mere duty to fulfil. What we focus on is eventually what we reflect.

8. Love the church

Jesus loved the church and gave himself for it (Eph 5:25). Can we do any less?

When we speak of the church we are often referring to its structures, meetings, officers, culture and growth, or lack of it. But the church is people, like you and me, with gifts and skills, faults and failings.

All relationships tend to go through three stages. First there is the veneer stage where we are nicer than God himself. The second stage is disillusionment with one another. The third stage is where we either opt out or we reaffirm our commitment to one another in our disillusionment. Love—God's love—takes us through the tough times.

As has been said so often, there is no perfect church, but should you find it, don't join it for you will ruin it!

R.A. Torrey, the brilliant preacher, once proclaimed, 'The word of God alone will not break a self-righteous, proud person. You will have to get him or her into the presence of God.' His presence is so often found in his body, the church.

Jim Cymala from the USA once noted, 'The Christian church was not born in a clever sermon but in a prayer meeting.' A church prayer meeting.

R.A. Torrey would be the first to note that Christ's presence is among his people. It *can* be found in the beauty of creation, of course, but his love, compassion and strong but gentle truth are seen and experienced among his people. Jim Cymala's comment is important in as much as a clever sermon can be put together by one person, whereas a prayer meeting involves many.

Despite my often hilarious or angry comments about it, I have always loved the church. My quips and some would say outbursts have more to do with errant bishops, outdated structures, self-indulgent corporate behaviour and a lack of passion for Scripture, truth and the lost. The tragedy is that people are in these structures, deluded and divorced from Scripture. But if we do not love people, we are out of line with Christ.

Believe me, I know the church can hurt you. I have been hurt over and over again. Twenty-five years of full-time pastoral work do not leave me with merely happy memories. I have been let down, lied about, dismissed, criticised and defrauded. But the love of Christ not only surpasses all understanding, but all misunderstanding as well!

One of my fine ex-secretaries has a daughter who eventually married an attractive young man. Problems set in, and another woman was involved, but she stood firm, despite the shame of a fractured marriage. Her husband lost faith, but she stayed in the church. Recently, after a Sunday evening meeting, I gave an appeal for those who wanted to start again, as God was 'the God of the second chance'. To my absolute shock, my ex-secretary's daughter and husband were not only in the meeting, but they were at the front before I had finished the appeal, both in tears. He had not met with us for at least two years. I did not know what to say, so I left the platform, went up to him and put my arms around him. He sobbed like a baby. He was almost in convulsions. Love is more than a feeling, as I have already said, but a touch or an embrace is often more eloquent than any words we can say. His response helped me love the church a little more. I was helped to understand Christ's love for us all, despite our waywardness. I confess this has little to do with me—it is the fruit of the Spirit, which reveals nothing but God's grace and mercy towards those of us who without him are selfish and self-seeking.

9. Assume personal responsibility

When we get something we have never had, we become responsible for something we have never done. I have often asked the Lord to help me see people the way he sees them, and I have found that as he does, I become responsible for things I have never done.

Two or three years ago I asked the Lord to help me see people in my own town, south west of London, as he sees them. I was reminded, by God's Spirit, that this would be difficult since I never saw those people—I was always busy at local planning meetings, national planning meetings, conferences small and large, making videos and teaching cassettes, writing books and counselling those already saved. My leisure time was spent with a few key trusted individuals and couples, all of whom were Christians.

So I began to decline invitations that a few years previously I would have regarded as indicative of success. I endeavoured graciously to say 'no' to invitations from international figures who invited me to their churches and conferences in America, South Africa, Malaysia and Australia. For what? To get to know my neighbours. I had to assume personal responsibility for my road, because if I didn't, who would? That required me to take time to walk down my road, pray for each household and see people as Christ sees them. It required my wife and me to invite our neighbours in for supper and drinks, and to take an interest in some of their lives, rather than simply expect them to take an interest in our faith. After a couple of years I feel I have joined the human race again!

Some of us need to take responsibility in the local church. It lacks commitment because we are not committed. It lacks love because we are not loving. It lacks care because we are not caring. It lacks concern for the lost because we do not demonstrate a concern for the lost.

Ignorance is overcome by truth.

Tradition is overcome by obedience.
Fear is overcome by love.

The road to the future starts here

In the mid-1800s a Scottish minister was asked to resign from his position. The church was not growing and few had made public responses to Christ. Eventually he returned home without a job or proper income.

At home he cared for a young man by the name of Robert, despite his economic hardship. Many years later, Robert was lecturing at an English university. 'I saw the smoke of 1,000 African villages who have never heard the gospel. Someone must go,' he preached. Sitting in that meeting was a man by the name of David Livingstone. 'I will go,' he replied.

Robert was none other than Robert Moffatt, now regarded as the father of overseas mission. He translated the Scriptures into many different languages.

The minister could have become bitter and resentful, comparing his lack of gifts with others, and he could have reacted against the harshness and apparent merciless behaviour of the Church Board. But instead he went on caring and loving, and he assumed personal responsibility for what was in his hands. As a result, through the discipleship of Robert Moffatt, he touched nations and probably millions of people.

While he was alive, few were concerned about David Livingstone, but when he died the King requested his body be shipped back and buried in Westminster Abbey. The night before his body left Africa, his loyal followers cut his heart out and buried it where it belonged—in African soil.

An unknown Scottish minister and a young lad named Robert. It looked so unimpressive.

Actions unnoticed by those who live in the present are nevertheless noted by the great Book Keeper.

Whatever our present situation, we must understand that what happens *in* us is more important than what happens *to* us. It affects the present. And that affects the future.

7

The Future

Beware when you take on the Church of God. Others have tried and have bitten the dust.

Archbishop Desmond Tutu

Looking to the future

As we look into the future with God several things will become apparent.

1. *We need to embrace God's vision for the earth*

He has not abandoned the cosmos, and his commitment to the peoples on the globe is fully expressed in his Son Jesus Christ. Jesus' best friend John tells us that he did not come into the world to judge it but to save it (Jn 3:17). That vision, rooted in Scripture and nourished by the Spirit, must be held clearly amid the myths, fantasies and illusions of twentieth-century life. Therefore must ask God either to give us fresh vision and help us to embrace it, or to sharpen our vision, as it can be lost in the fog of the multitude of activities, pleasures and appointments that invade us continually.

If we want to be people with a future then we must have a vision for it.

2. We have to be ready to embark upon a mission

It is the difference between nomads and pilgrims. Nomads travel, simply wandering from place to place, whereas pilgrims are on a journey with a purpose. This demands sacrifice, perseverance and tenacity. Nomads are happy to be going nowhere and are expecting nothing but survival. Jesus Christ is our model for mission. It is fulfilled in our network of relationships at home, the area in which we live—with those who know the Lord and those who as yet do not know him. It can be rooted in geography or a special people group such as children or youth, the unemployed or business people. Mission is the means through which the heavenly vision will be fulfilled.

3. We have to count the cost

If aspirations are to be turned to achievements, there will be a cost factor. This is true of every area of life. It is not unique to the Christian world. The cost of having children involves sacrifice and disappointment. The cost of faithfulness is embracing the pain of reality rather than the painlessness of fantasy. While we may never fully understand the cost of walking with Christ throughout the whole of our lives, he gives grace for each day.

Counting the cost will prepare us for the adversities of life.

4. We have to face the opposition

Anything worth while will be opposed. To think otherwise is foolishness. The enemy of the best is the good. The enemy of light is darkness. The enemy of creativity is mediocrity. Thank God that for most of us there are places to which we can retire to replenish our energies, find encouragement and prepare ourselves for war.

Facing the opposition will teach us the power of love, servanthood, faith and truth. It prepares us for the age to come.

5. We need to take action in the present

Too many of us are either looking over our shoulders at the past, which debilitates our strength, or we are longingly hoping for a better future. But our actions in the present will determine how much of our past will affect us now and how many of our future dreams will become realities.

Nostalgia or romanticism can rob us of a future where our lives will become meaningful, influential and purposeful. It is important in the age of individualism that we understand the nature of the body of Christ, friendships and relationships. We are unlikely to fulfil this vision and accomplish our mission on our own. Every biblical figure of worth and renown found this to be true. Salvation is free—there is nothing we can do to earn it—but there is a prize to be won, and that demands effort and energy in the here and now.

What of the future?

How much of the future is there left?

A scientific journal recently suggested that the earth could be hit by a shower of asteroids, doing untold damage and perhaps even knocking us out of orbit! The end may come in an altogether different way as the nuclear arsenal is developed without checks and balances, and warheads criss-cross through the skies to make life on earth virtually impossible. The end will be accelerated through global pollution and using up the resources of the earth in an ever-increasing frenzy to satisfy personal ambition and the pleasure syndrome.

But for all of us the question can be answered somewhat more bluntly. Each of us will die, irrespective of global warfare or pollution, extra-terrestrial activity or disease.

Every reader may have another ten or fifty years, but one thing we can be sure of is that we *shall* die. For each one of us that is how much of the future there is left.

Here for a moment

Most scientists, whether they be Christians or not, are in agreement that we live in a very old universe. We are part of an old solar system, and the planet on which we live is millions of years old. One scientist suggested that if we take the height of a monument such as Cleopatra's Needle on London's Embankment and we compare that to the age of the earth, and then measure up alongside it the time human beings have been on the earth, we would have to put a coin alongside it. In terms of the age of our globe, the solar system and the universe, we have been here but for a moment.

The Apostle Paul had a good perspective on time. After years of beatings, imprisonment, being half drowned and shipwrecked, hungry and thirsty he called it a 'slight momentary affliction' (2 Cor 4:17, RSV). He saw his life as a 'moment'.

Perhaps Paul's moment put all of his successes and failures into perspective. It shaped his present world-view and therefore determined his future.

There are many things which can hinder us from

fulfilling our vision and mission. To sum up, I believe we can call these diversions.

There are two sorts of diversions. There are legitimate diversions and illegitimate diversions. But they are both diversions!

If I go to speak at a conference and set off at 5 pm on a two-hour journey for a meeting that starts at 7.30 pm, that is reasonable. If I leave at 5 pm and rob a bank on the way, I think we could safely say that was an illegitimate diversion for a Christian leader! But equally, if I stop for a three-course meal—something that is not illegal or illegitimate—that is a diversion. It will hinder me from getting there on time and fulfilling my mission. The enemy wants to divert us, and I know of so many kind, sincere and often passionate but frustrated people who do not realise they have been diverted.

Discouragement can be a major diversion. I become discouraged when I realise how powerless we in our Pioneer network of churches have been in reaching out to the lost. So often we come back to pastoral and care issues which, though vital, can hinder us from even relating to the unconverted, never mind seeing them become disciples of Christ.

There are many things that discourage us, and that is when we are likely to take a short- or long-term diversion. It may be legitimate or illegitimate, but it is still a diversion and will affect our future and maybe the future of others.

What do you know?

The future, then, must not be determined by the doom and gloom around us, either at home or overseas. That darkness should tenderise our hearts and focus our minds on the fact that our future on this earth is limited—it is but a 'moment'. We have been equipped through Christ's death and resurrection to shine as lights in the darkness. The love of God overcomes the fear of death. We need have no fear that our 'moment' will become meaningless and irrelevant to God. Therefore we need not take diversions, but even if we do, a change of heart leads to a change of direction, and we can find ourselves back in the grace and mercy of God, who will say, 'This is the way; walk in it' (Is 30:21).

The Apostle Paul made it clear that even the prophetic church will only 'know' in part (1 Cor 13:9). And that includes our past and our future. We don't know how long we are going to live, and we don't know where we will be politically, culturally or relationally in ten or twenty years' time. What is important is that we are people who look for opportunities in potential problems rather than problems in potential opportunities. Otherwise we will be continually discouraged.

Future tense?

Discouragement often turns to depression. Depression leads to comparing ourselves with others, and this in turn leads to self-pity, resentment and bitterness. Many are bitter but do not know it. Bitterness is not something you wake up with one day—it is a process that often starts with discouragement and ends up with a clenched fist in the heart.

King Saul started so well, but ended up a suicidal maniac! He went through discouragement, comparing himself with others and abusing his position, and as a result self-gratification and self-fulfilment became his motivation. He became a walking disaster area.

I often wonder what would have happened if Saul had walked with God. What would have happened to Joseph if he had not foolishly shared his vision of the future in pride and superiority? What would have happened to Samson if he had not had a problem with the opposite sex which resulted in him having his hair cut off? God was not responsible for those major areas of disobedience and sin. They were the choices of the individuals, and their future was radically affected as a result. God, in his grace, brought good out of those situations, but that was his grace and sovereignty; it may have had little to do with his original plan.

Revival or destruction?

As we look at the lives of biblical figures and the decisions they made, those decisions meant either revival or destruction for them. So it is with us.

Those of us in the first world (so-called civilised nations) are not living in revival. God has poured out his Spirit in answer to the prayers of millions in South America, Africa, China, Romania and many other nations saddled with colossal economic and health problems. There is a worldwide revival going on, but North America and Western Europe are at the tail end of it.

However, there are keys to personal revival, which can be the prelude to corporate revival of the church, which in turn will spill out into a great awakening in the nations.

Keys to revival

Christian sociologists, statisticians and observers are agreed that revival situations and church growth situations have four major keys.

1. Fellowship

This is more than friendliness. It is deeper than friendliness. In the New Testament its common use is related to a 'willingness to give and share' (*New Bible Dictionary*, IVP). The emphasis is on a participation in something rather than association with others. I suggest that the 'something' is related to the historic and concrete acts of Christ's birth, life, death and resurrection, which we are invited to participate in and have fellowship in.

Fellowship, the participation in fellowship with God himself which leads us to fellowship with others, is going to be vital as we look into the future.

Ruthless dictators, inept and corrupt politicians, a disintegrating monarchy, massive two-thirds world debt, a soaring crime rate, threats from within and without are the inevitable outcomes of abandoning God. According to the British *Times* newspaper, the USA is heading for a two-thirds world economy within a decade or two. They reckon it is irreversible, and there will be a 6 trillion dollar debt.

To bring it home even closer, many of us feel unsafe on the streets. Our homes have been broken into and so have our vehicles. In Britain men as well as women have been raped on trains and robbed and raped in parks! If it is true that HIV will eventually claim between 30 and 40 million lives within the next decade or so, each of us will know of somebody who is HIV-positive.

If we escape the pressures of the scenario I have just

outlined, we should be grateful. But we will be surrounded by those who have not been able to make
such an escape. Those coming to Christ will have their
own major personal problems and histories as well as
the scenario I have outlined to cope with. Many don't
cope, and the suicide rate in many parts of the world is
on the increase. This includes those in prisons and
borstals, and not a few who have been made redundant
or bankrupt.

While we should thank God for Scripture and the
presence of his Holy Spirit in our lives, I say with
reverence that they are insufficient and inadequate to
give us the help we need. That is why, when we are
converted to Christ, we are put in a body which is called
the church. Christian fellowship encourages and affirms.
It gives us fresh perspectives that release us from the
doom and gloom scenario, and equip us to let our light
shine in that darkness.

Fellowship helps us understand we are not in this
alone. We don't have to carry the state of the world,
and the part that we relate to, on our own. Fellowship
gives us options, and stops us being shut up with our
own perspectives. Fellowship also enables us to laugh,
eat and drink with those we love and trust, which
recharges our batteries and equips us to be effective
agents of the kingdom. Laughter destroys fear.

It has been said that people are remembered for one of
two things: (a) the problems they create; or (b) the
problems they resolve.

People who are continually creating problems are not
in fellowship and they are probably hurt. Hurt people
hurt more people. But those resolving problems are
normally in fellowship and co-operation with others.

If we are to be saved from irrelevancy we must

reaffirm our commitment to the things that Christ is committed to. That includes human relationships—especially those in the household of faith.

A while back I wrote to a national Christian magazine saying that I had a list of eminent Christian leaders who don't go to church and I suggested that it should be published in the magazine. They declined. As I knew the editor he probably wondered whether it was some sort of joke. Had he agreed, I am not sure I would have supplied him with the list, but it is of great concern to me that we have a number of Christian leaders who write books, make tapes and appear on television who don't go to church and in that sense are not in fellowship, other than with those working under their care. They can't be challenged and probably cannot be befriended.

God has made us for friendship and fellowship, whereas the enemy always wants to isolate us. The result of this is that we now have a massive social problem in our world where extreme emotional immaturity masquerades as an adult lifestyle. However, the great thing with God is that it is not important where we have been, but it is important to know where we are going. Going it alone is not God's intention nor part of God's plan. If we have not learned how to relate and have fellowship we have failed to understand the nature of our salvation.

From God's perspective faithfulness in fellowship precedes success in ministry. We cannot separate Christianity from the church; the medium is indeed the message.

Fellowship, friendship, partnership, co-operation and a sense of togetherness and purpose—all of these form a major key to a future filled with effectiveness and even revival.

2. Worship and prayer

What we feed on determines our future. Some feed off one another, griping and complaining, pointing out the inadequacies and deficiencies of the church and sowing seeds of discontent. That will determine people's future. All of us have reason to complain, but there is a process for grievances.

Feeding off Christ involves worship and prayer.

Worship is not for God's benefit alone. There is a sense in which he does not need our worship, because there is no inadequacy in the Godhead. He isn't lonely, bored or egotistically demanding that we worship him. He is a God of grace and humility, even towards those who treat him badly.

No, worship is primarily for us! As music plays it allows our minds to be renewed and our hearts to be warmed, and it causes us to see things from a fresh perspective. It allows us to get in touch with heaven and heaven to get in touch with us.

Worship is basically prayer put to music. Worship—that sense of togetherness in words and music—is a vital key to keeping our hearts clean, our minds focused and our relationships nurtured. As we read through the Psalms it is clear the psalmists sang to God, they sang to one another, they sang to creation and they sang of their enemies. It was a much broader perspective than we often experience in church.

Being children of promise we are given many promises. These come through Scripture regarding the age to come, our eternal reward and gaining the prize. But with the increasing amount of prophetic ministry there are also promises made, many of which are to do with the here and now or the here and not-too-distant future! But it seems to me, reading through Scripture, that when God promises 'milk and honey' he often then leads us through a desert experience. It is at such times that these two important keys—fellowship and worship—are so valuable and important.

If fellowship, togetherness and purpose provide an emotional support system and give us significance, worship allows us to be reminded that God has not left us on our own. The words of Scripture remind us of God's faithfulness.

I appreciate that in some circles people are in danger of singing themselves into oblivion. Lengthy times of worship, led because 'that's what we do in our church', will in fact devalue worship. Occasionally, when I sit through a very lengthy time of worship that doesn't have a great deal of anointing or purpose I am reminded of the verse, 'They sang a hymn and they went out!' This can sound very inviting!

There is no doubt, however, that vision and mission are nurtured by fellowship and sustained in an anointed, worshipping atmosphere. Conservative Evangelicals hardly ever talk about anointing—it has been largely relegated to Old Testament prophets and kings. But there is no doubt that wherever there is fresh vision, revival or awakening, worship is playing a major key, whether it be in Africa, South America or now, thank God, in parts of the Western world. There is a presence in worship—an anointing whereby faith is increased, vision becomes focused and life's troubles are seen in perspective.

It is not unusual for some of the younger men in the Pioneer network of churches who lead churches or training initiatives to ask if they can travel with me. Sometimes it will be for a few days away in the UK or overseas. On other occasions it is simply to benefit from an hour or two's drive to and from a venue so that we can talk and fellowship and so that they can look at how I am doing and maybe learn a little something from my experience.

On one occasion I travelled to the north of England with one of our young men to speak at one or two townwide meetings. Early one morning I was awoken to loud sounds of singing in tongues! Wondering what was going on, I poked my head out of the bedroom window and realised that somebody was in the shower singing praises to God. Although we were in the home of Christian people I found myself embarrassed, despite the fact that we were off to a Sunday morning meeting within a couple of hours. I was brought a cup of coffee by the man of the house and it was clear he had not been in the shower. He explained that his wife would be getting up soon to cook us breakfast, so she couldn't have been the culprit either. It had to be the young man who had asked to come with me!

We went through our meetings and travelled on to another place. That night we were in another home and once again I could hear him praying and speaking in tongues, though this time he was aware that folk had retired to bed and he was therefore a little quieter. But the next morning exactly the same thing happened: loud singing and praising in tongues.

This was a great challenge to me. I love worship. But I realised over that weekend that although I was a very good corporate worshipper, I had lost some of the personal aspects of worship. I remembered the times I used to walk around my garden singing, or go off for a little drive to walk in the fields and the woods to worship God, to bless him and to gain fresh perspectives. That weekend challenged my own need to develop personal worship. I had taught that corporate worship will only be as good as personal worshippers. Of course there are exceptions to that: those weighed down with the affairs of life come into a worshipping atmosphere and slowly that oppression lifts and they then become worshippers themselves.

Thank God for fellowship which challenges by example and urges us on to better things. I know I have become a better worshipper as a result of that weekend. The young man travelled to learn from me, but I learned so much from him.

Worship and prayer form the environment of the Spirit-filled person and the Spirit-filled church. Paul makes it clear that one of the primary ways of being filled with the Spirit is to 'speak to one another with psalms, hymns and spiritual songs. Sing and make music in your heart to the Lord' (Eph 5:19).

3. Liberty of the Spirit

Jonathan Edwards was only fifty-five when he died. Perry Miller called him 'the greatest philosopher/theologian yet to grace the American scene'. It was under his preaching that the Great Awakening took place in the USA between 1734 and 1735. (A more extensive revival took place in 1740–41.) A firm friend of George Whitefield, he was of the tradition of the New England Calvinists. In fact it was noted that he was agitated by Arminianism.

Most churches and church leaders who would like to be known as Calvinists or Reformed would be strong on exegetical teaching and firmly opposed to anything regarded as 'emotional', including clapping, dancing, laughing in worship or being 'slain in the Spirit'. They are known for emphasising reverence for Christ and Scripture and decorum in all matters corporate.

Nevertheless, when writing about the things he saw under his ministry, Jonathan Edwards observed: 'The apostolic times seem to have returned upon us, such a display has there been of the power and the grace of the Spirit.' He goes on to speak of 'extraordinary affections, of fear, sorrow, desire, love, of joy, tears, of trembling, of groans, loud cries and agonies of the body'. He adds that he also saw 'the failing of bodily strength'. He wrote, 'We are all ready to own that no man can see God and live. If we then even see a small part of the love and glory of Christ, a very foretaste of heaven, is it any wonder that our bodily strength is diminished?'

Now this is the sort of thing you might expect from Arminians. Who are Arminians? Well, they are often overlooked, despite being an important part of the Reformation, and they are sometimes called 'Radical Reformists'. In the sixteenth century they wanted to abolish the practices and traditions of the mediaeval Roman Catholic Church and build up a church entirely on New Testament principles. They were pacifists, and they called for the separation of church and state, emphasising the fact that Christ died for all (not the elected few) and that God's saving grace is not irresistible. They therefore contended that it is possible for those who are Christians to fall from grace. In their return to the New Testament and a somewhat different view of Scripture, their more informal approach paved the way for what many regard to be a far greater degree of liberty in fellowship, worship, in many cases gifts of the Holy Spirit and in an overall lifestyle.

Thus both Calvinists and Arminians have experienced emotional manifestations accompanying revival.

At the time of writing (summer 1994) there has been an unusual series of events happening in America, Canada, the UK and other parts of Europe. It is marked by people collapsing in meetings and laying seemingly unconscious for up to an hour at a time. Uproarious laughter is accompanied by tears, kneeling and people prostrating themselves in worship. There have been violent demonic manifestations alongside what many regard to be 'a taste of heaven'.

Rodney Howard-Browne, a South African who was an associate of Ray McCauley of the Rhema Church in Johannesburg, settled in America in 1987. He had often known what he called a 'fresh anointing' under his ministry. This sometimes resulted in people breaking into laughter or tears. There were others whose 'bodily strength failed them'. Like others before him, that anointing strengthened but then diminished. He told an audience in June 1994 that this may have been because it would have been like giving 'a shotgun to a four-year-old'. But in recent years people from a wide range of backgrounds have ended up in his meetings in a state that can only be described as 'drunk' in the Holy Spirit, with bodily strength failing them, while others all around are roaring with laughter or are in tears of joy or repentance.

At one of his meetings in Tulsa he laid hands on Randy Clark, a Vineyard leader. Randy visited Toronto with this new anointing which the leaders of Airport Vineyard Toronto were keen to give away. From January 1994 up to the time of writing they have been meeting six nights a week (Mondays are off!) to pray with people for a fresh anointing, with times marked by holy laughter, tears of repentance and people whose bodily strength fails them. According to one first-hand observer, thousands of clergy and leaders from various parts of the world have flown in to be refreshed in the presence of the Lord.

I have no doubt whatever that those who honour what God has done, but are likely to resist what he is currently doing, will make this one of the most controversial issues of our times.

A personal testimony

Unaware of this new-found liberty in Rodney Howard-Browne's meetings in Toronto (and now in hundreds of places that have been touched by this new liberty), a pattern was building up in my own ministry.

Despite a good week at England's Spring Harvest in 1994 with some 6,000 people, I have to say that nothing extraordinary took place. People were touched by the Holy Spirit, there were a few prophetic words given and a number came to Christ. I then went to Dublin and spoke at a seminar on handling prophets and prophecy which, as it turns out, they have told many was the best thing they had ever heard on the subject. I was somewhat bemused, for although I was grateful for their kind comments to me, it was just another good event. But that night over 1,000 packed into an auditorium, and after a wonderful time worshipping the Lord, I gave teaching about kingdom issues. The front of the auditorium was flooded with scores and scores of people visibly moved by the Holy Spirit. Many were in tears, others dropped on their knees and two or three were literally rolling around the floor in laughter. I went down to pray with people and their 'bodily strength was failing them' in droves!

I moved on to Geneva thinking, 'Well, that is what the Lord was doing in Dublin.' Hundreds of leaders gathered in Geneva for what turned out to be a very special time of worship and teaching, with strong prophetic words for individuals and many touched in similar ways by the Holy Spirit.

Returning to another week of Spring Harvest, although it was a good week it has to be said that the same things were not happening there. Although I was aware that something unique was taking place, I was not yet seeing a pattern throughout that month of April.

In May I went to speak in Orebro, Sweden, with John Paul Jackson, who has been linked with John Wimber. The worship, I confess, was anointed and there was a certain purity and innocence about those who led us. The teaching from John Paul and myself seemed to be appreciated. But what stood out more than anything else was a strong anointing which left many people flat on their backs for up to an hour and leaders of churches literally crawling around on their hands and knees, unable to stand on their own two feet. It was impossible to finish meetings (and after a coffee break start again) as the whole day blended into one long event!

That same month I went to John Mumford's Vineyard Church in South West London. It was a sunny morning as I drove into the hired school premises. I enjoyed the worship and the banter that took place from the platform to the congregation. Warmth and humour, worship and prayer made my speaking task easy. At the close there was a good response. I prayed over a number of people and gave some specific words from the Lord, which drew a remarkable response from John Mumford as we lunched together afterwards. 'We have never seen such power on a Sunday morning!' To me it had been another good meeting and God had been present. Slowly I was becoming aware that a pattern was building up.

I then went with my close friend and travelling colleague Noel Richards to Frankfurt, but Noel had lost his voice. It was important he did not sing over the weekend as he was recording a brand new album 'Warrior' the following week. To overcome this difficulty he played a CD over the PA system to the 200 leaders from around Frankfurt who gathered for the seminars. Most had no idea he was miming—they thought he was simply singing to backing tracks. Within a short space of time leaders were first on their knees and then prostrate before the Lord, some weeping and others filled with the awe of the Lord. I couldn't believe it: Noel was miming and God was blessing! Accurate words of knowledge were given which only the church could have known about, and then without any provocation or indeed any stories about Rodney Howard-Browne, Toronto, or what was happening elsewhere in my own ministry, several women sitting on the floor began roaring with laughter. They laughed and laughed and laughed! Rudi Pinke, the main leader of the church in Frankfurt, told me afterwards that one of the women had nothing to laugh about. She was seriously ill and was going blind. It made it even more wonderful.

I have no doubt whatever that this new-found liberty will deeply offend the religious establishment—even the evangelical religious establishment. As it was in Bible days, it is inevitable that where the Holy Spirit is at work, the flesh and the devil will also be at work. If the worst the flesh does is to laugh in meetings or to weep in repentance, I for one will be quite happy! It is also inevitable that where there is a strong presence of God the demonic will make itself known.

It was said that Jonathan Edwards was 'a complete stranger to that separation of heart and head that has often plagued evangelical religion'. I have chosen to use the Jonathan Edwards stories and narratives as I believe God wants to bring a new Spirit of liberty to his church, much of which has been deeply influenced by Calvinism, with its high view of Scripture and its suspicion of most things emotional.

I can only conclude that what matters in the final analysis is not the manifestation but the fruit.

It was in June when I flew back from Frankfurt and my colleague Martin Scott was speaking at our Sunday evening meeting. Both of us were aware that God was wanting to break into our church in a fresh way. It would also be the fulfilment of prophetic ministry given to our church in May 1990, which I wrote about at the conclusion of my autobiography *An Intelligent Fire*.

4. A care for the lost

From what I have read of revival, whether it be a personal revival or a corporate revival, one of the hallmarks has been the care for people who are unchurched.

It would seem, as it was with the church in Corinth, that manifestations of the Holy Spirit, glossolalia and even extraordinary miracles can, unless properly led, cause one's eyes to be taken off Christ and his mission and placed firmly onto the phenomena. Meetings are judged by laughter and tears, bodies on the floor or strange happenings.

I have been in more than one situation where there have been extraordinary things happening over a period of time. But my concern is that there is a self-indulgence—a power for power's sake.

I remember being at a large event with many thousands of people where I was playing a small part. Afterwards two or three people exclaimed, 'What power?' as people were virtually lying in heaps on the stage. But nobody had the courage to ask, 'Why?' In other words, 'Why is this power being given?'

Our God is a purposeful God and he doesn't come among his people simply to entertain them. His blessing is purposeful. Personal revival that does not lead to corporate revival is an act of grace, but it will fall short of God's intentions. Corporate revival, holy laughter and tears, people's strength failing them and Holy Spirit drunkenness are all found in Scripture. But they can turn 'in and down' and become a remarkable novelty.

The Apostle John, Jesus' best friend, summed up the purposefulness of heaven in the well-known verse found in his Gospel, where we are told that God so loved the cosmos that he *gave* his Son. Today, in an environment where people are wanting to 'get' blessed, refreshed and quite understandably revived, the ultimate intention must be that we then take that blessing and 'give' to the rest of the church and to those who are still lost, as we once were.

Back to Scripture

By the time you get to read this chapter, the phenomena of laughter and tears, Holy Spirit drunkenness and the like will be all over Britain. It will have hit Anglican churches and New Churches, Pentecostal churches and indeed all sorts of churches. But these phenomena are

not new. We should never forget that the reason Paul
wrote to the church in Corinth was because the leadership had a 'hands off' view of the work of the Holy
Spirit. There were clear manifestations of the Holy
Spirit in tongues and prophecy and a wide range of
other phenomena, but there was also the flesh! Outside
the meetings there was immorality; they were taking
each other to court and suing each other; there was a
great deal of greed and selfishness, even around the
Lord's table. I have often read Paul's first letter to
Corinth and asked, 'In God's name what were the
elders doing?' It appears they were doing nothing.
They were just letting it all happen, giving no instruction to the church as to what was of God, what was of
the flesh and what was of the devil. The less discerning
even became caught up in this revival atmosphere and
would have been steadily deceived into imagining that
all this was acceptable. It was not!

Leadership therefore has a responsibility to ensure
that the activity of the Holy Spirit is properly admini-
strated. What do I mean by that? In Corinth they had
lots of tongues in meetings, many of which were not
interpreted. So Paul was very practical. He didn't say
they must stop speaking in tongues, but neither did he
leave it to go on. He said in effect that three tongues in a
meeting was enough! Was he quenching the Spirit? No,
he was simply administrating the work of God in a way
that would cause it to be Christ-centred and less self-
indulgent.

Therefore we as leaders have a role to explain to the
church what is of the Spirit, what is probably of the flesh
and what is demonic. The answer to the one-man ministry is not the every-person-doing-their-own-thing ministry. In most of his letters the Apostle Paul expressed

the need for caution and wisdom with the activity of the Holy Spirit and people's response to the Holy Spirit. Even leaders were told not to lay hands on people too soon.

There are a number of people like Billy Graham, Reinhard Bonnke, Ray McCauley, John Stott, Michael Green and Rodney Howard-Browne whom I would love to lay hands on me. I want what they have got. But there are others about whom quite frankly I have to say I don't want what they have got!

What fills you up eventually gets out! So we have a responsibility to ensure that there is a 'hands on' approach to this work and that it is turned 'up and out' and wisely directed in a way that will mean that liberty remains a hallmark of God's work, but divine order ensures that we are here for the long haul not the short sprint.

The present activity of the Holy Spirit in many churches will come and go. Leadership will be unable to incorporate the liberty of the Spirit into their church structures. They will simply add on an extra meeting for those who want to be refreshed. Praise God for that. But unless it affects our structures, we will have two churches running along in parallel: the church filled with the Holy Spirit, signs and wonders and phenomena, and the other church which carries on pretty well as normal.

There will be others who leave their church structures (which will be another bone of colossal contention) in order to follow the Spirit. They will find that leaving their denomination is sometimes seen as far worse than adultery or homosexuality. It is a very costly business when you want to follow the Spirit who will not be allowed into your church structures.

But where the Holy Spirit is allowed to refresh individuals and then the corporate body of Christ (the local
church), Christ-honouring ministry will take place
which will spill out to the lost.

An awareness of sin, followed by repentance and acts
of reconciliation, is at the heart of every move of God.
But this is not simply for the Christian community, as
our acts of sin are often directed against unbelievers,
intentionally and unintentionally. For some it is simply
the sin of not sharing our faith with the lost, albeit in a
sensitive and kindly fashion.

The Salvation Army

During the DAWN (Discipling a Whole Nation) conference at Birmingham in the spring of 1992 the Lord gave
me a prophecy for the Salvation Army. I do not recall
ever having any sort of relationship with the organisation before, or with any key leaders in it. Phil Wall,
whom I barely knew, was perhaps my only contact.

The prophetic word spoke of a new day coming to the
Salvation Army, God's breath sweeping through it, that
they would touch the Royal Family and those sleeping
out in the streets; and that God would give them great
wisdom with regard to using the uniform in some
situations and dispensing with it in others.

As I prophesied in tears before the 700 leaders gathered from every major denomination, something else
was going on. It was like a tape running in my head.
'I don't believe in all this—men and women dressing up
in uniforms, calling each other Major or Colonel, pran-
cing around playing bands.' My emotions were going in
one direction concerning the heart of God for the Salvation Army, but my mind was going in another. Faced

with this dichotomy I felt the Lord say to me, 'Thank you very much for your opinions, Gerald. I just don't need them at the moment.'

At the close of the evening, senior officers came to me in tears asking, 'Do you think God will give us another opportunity?' I confess I was surprised and humbled at their response, as I hadn't been sure whether they even understood prophecy, never mind whether they would receive it.

Two years later I received an invitation to speak at the Salvation Army Evangelists Conference. Michael Green spoke brilliantly to over 300 officers and those in training. He spoke on evangelism: motive, methods and flexibility. I was to speak on the Saturday evening, and by then the air of expectancy was incredible, and I confess I was nervous as John Dangerfield welcomed me and I began to speak. The Lord gave great grace to both speaker and listeners, and I asked all the officers to come and stand at the front of the platform.

I had been sent some olive oil from Jerusalem, and I suggested to Michael Green that we anoint these officers for a new move of God in the Salvation Army. As they stood at the front, Michael and I took the olive oil and anointed each one, briefly commenting and praying over them. Two or three began to cry, but it was a fairly quiet time for the majority of those who were still sitting in their chairs. A pianist was playing quietly, but there was nobody on the platform, and there was no ministry taking place in the body of the conference. The men and women sat and watched a row of backs, while Michael and I quietly moved along the line. Suddenly, without warning, one of the men began to shake and jump around in his chair. Others dropped to their knees, and some were overwhelmed with the Spirit of God and began to smile and then to laugh. As Michael and I went round ministering to people—some sitting, others standing, and some now on the floor virtually unconscious—we were aware that something quite extraordinary was taking place.

One young man of eighteen prayed at my request for the pianist. The man was so overwhelmed by the Spirit that his fingers dropped from the keyboard, he slumped on his stool and then fell on to the floor, semi-conscious. Then he began to laugh. The eighteen-year-old stared at the palms of his hands, and then at the pianist lying on the floor laughing. His bewildered gaze went from one to the other, fascinated and bewildered that God should use him!

Many officers told me that night: 'We have never seen such things in all of our lifetime.' But Catherine Bramwell Booth wrote in her book *Echoes and Memories*:

All my life I have been interested in what are sometimes spoken of as bodily manifestations, though I have a considerable degree of misgivings. From my earliest years of responding to work for God I have approached all such manifestations, if not with a hostile mind, certainly with a mind deliberately cautious. I have always felt that anything claiming to be of the supernatural must have credentials which placed its genuinness beyond doubt. Nevertheless, I have this feeling also—and with regard to the Army I have particularly—that there is a place for these outward demonstrations which have undoubtedly been witnessed by us, and the like of which are recorded in various periods of religious history.

Referring to a case in her journal of 16th January 1878, Catherine wrote:

The power of the Holy Ghost fell on Robinson and prostrated him. But he nearly fainted twice. The brother of Blands entered into full liberty and then he shouted, wept, clapped his hands, danced and made a scene of the most glorious and heavenly enthusiasm. Others meanwhile were lying prostrate on the floor, some of them groaning aloud for perfect deliverance.

She concluded the chapter:

In the United States in the earlier days we had a record of somewhat similar experiences, except they generally took the form of extreme joy. One of the peculiarities of the prostrations and trances and the like in Europe has been the solemnity which has always marked their occurrence ... In these demonstrations of the Spirit, the reality of which no one would challenge who knew what had really happened, there was an accompaniment of overpowering joy, exhibited in singing, and sometimes in a disposition to dance or to remain for a long period in a kind of ecstasy.

A short time ago, one of the senior officers in the SA wrote and told me that the Saturday night conference meeting had been 'a watershed in the history of the Salvation Army'.

Looking up and reaching out

In the summer of 1994 I was invited to speak to the senior people in the New Covenant Ministries network of churches led by Bryn Jones. The major division in the New Churches (house churches) which took place in 1976 has been well documented by Dr Andrew Walker in his book *Restoring the Kingdom*. Within a decade there was a measure of reconciliation, but in real terms it simply meant that much of the hostility and rumour-mongering that went on diminished. There were few tangible expressions of repentance and reconciliation. So to get an invitation to speak to Bryn and his leaders was, in the minds of some, no minor miracle in itself. The Lord gave great grace as I spoke of a vision to see the nation networked with the gospel. There was a helpful time of questions and answers and then I began to share what God had been doing through Rodney Howard-Browne, the Toronto experience and churches in various parts of the country. At the close we decided to pray and there was a crescendo of praise and prayer which quite took me back. Within minutes there were people drunk in the Spirit on the floor, some crying, others laughing. One young man seemed not to be in the meeting at all and it was not affecting him. I went over and prayed with him and within a few moments he was shaking from head to toe and crying almost in convulsions. Within a few more minutes he was completely drunk in the Spirit and had collapsed in his chair. The following Thursday I had heard that that night he went home and led four people to Christ and by Thursday he had led eleven to Christ.

Another church leader went back to his town, explained to the church what was happening, had a time of waiting on God and they also had a divine visitation. This is a sizable church, strong and solid. The next day one of the older children came back and asked her father for four Bibles. Asking why, the father was told that she had led four friends to Christ! Somewhat astonished, the father asked what had happened. The girl, it seemed, had told her friends (in the toilet!) what had gone on in church the day before and they had fallen on the floor! The result was that they asked to 'see Jesus again' the next day!

One night a woman woke her husband up: 'God is

speaking to me. What are you up to? God is telling you you must repent.'

It turned out that her husband had committed adultery quite recently and had hidden it from his wife. There was an immediate confession of sin and the family are now being helped through all the implications and ramifications. This took place in one of our Pioneer churches.

A leader from one of the Pioneer network churches came to me and made confession of sexual sin which took place over ten years ago. The sin was confessed at the time to one or two mature Christians, repentance took place and it has not recurred since. So why bring it up again?

'It is simply the presence of God. I can't keep this from you any longer,' the leader said. This has resulted in a far greater openness in that church leadership. The man told me: 'For the first time in my life I feel clean, absolutely clean!'

These are the marks of the true work of God. It was the famous revivalist D.L. Moody who said, 'I believe that Pentecost was but a specimen day. I think the church has made this woeful mistake that Pentecost was a miracle never to be repeated.' On that day 3,000 came to Christ. Any move of God, any outpouring or refreshing from the Holy Spirit that does not reach out to the lost does not mean that God is at fault. Rather it means that we in our selfish, self-indulgent and fearful ways took the blessing to ourselves with no heart for the lost.

Dietrich Bonhoeffer commented, 'Unless we are the church for others we aren't the church at all.'

Revival, however, is heady stuff. Confession of sin, reconciliation, healings and stories of miraculous intervention can create quite an atmosphere, where terms of reference can be lost. We should never forget that Adam was in paradise when he sinned. Eve was in paradise when she was deceived. We should never forget that the devil was once worshipping God, singing his praises and was a skilled musician in a place of power and influence. Look at what he is doing today! He is causing the lost to remain lost.

But a declaration of the gospel—gossiping the gospel truth in one-to-one conversations—along with signs and wonders, is creating the biggest harvest the world has ever seen. Every day tens of thousands of people are coming to Christ, and most of them are experiencing that in an atmosphere of faith, signs and wonders.

Who's wondering?

Signs are to point people to something other than the sign. Signs of a supernatural order cause people to wonder. It happened in Jesus' ministry and throughout the New Testament. But Christian people are not the ones who are supposed to be doing the wondering! We are meant to have some idea of what is going on.

Hosea prophesied that our Lord 'will come to us like the winter rains, like the spring rains that water the earth'. Maybe he picked up the idea (prophets interpreting prophets?) from Moses when he said, '[He] will send rain on your land in its season, both autumn and spring rains that you may gather in your grain, new wine and oil' (Deut 11:13–14).

When God's people entered the promised land he told them about those early and later rains: spring for planting, autumn for reaping.

We are at a time of reaping. It is harvest time!

It has been pointed out that when Peter stood up on the Day of Pentecost and explained, 'This is what was spoken by the prophet Joel' (Acts 2:16), the literal translation is, 'This is the *beginning* of that which was spoken by the prophet Joel.' On that day 3,000 people were converted and became followers of Christ. Today there is a colossal outpouring of the Holy Spirit all over the world as the gospel is preached and nations are soaked in prayer.

Caught in a quandary

In the West we have lived with the social analysis of Karl Marx, the philosophy of Friedrich Nietzsche, the psychology of Sigmund Freud and the biology of Charles Darwin. Between them, to quote another, 'This is a fine mess you've gotten me into!'

It is now time for a new Spirit, the Holy Spirit, to prepare the church for her future. When you are God you can work anywhere you want to, but God, it seems, works best where he is most welcome; where his word is preached and there is a spirit of servanthood; where there is an openness to the Spirit as well as the word.

The old adage sums up the situation rather well:

The word without the Spirit will make you dry up.
The Spirit without the word will make you blow up.
The Spirit and the word together will make you grow up.

Our future begins now. What you have just read is past. The future begins here. We need to put ourselves under the flow of God's Spirit; in the way of his love and goodness. It is the goodness and kindness of God that causes a change of heart.

But there are some questions we need to ask with humility.

On 25th June 1994 in 176 nations, over 10 million Christians took to the streets to declare that the earth is the Lord's and all that is in it. It is Christians who will come out of their homes and out of their church buildings and who are willing to be identified publicly for Christ who are the most likely through their lives, communication, preaching and teaching to communicate the gospel.

As the angels looked on never before had they seen the earth filled with millions of its inhabitants who were standing together and marching together around the globe for the Creator and Saviour. What a sight it must have been!

So how much of the future is there left? These are the end times, but are they the end of the end times? That is the big question.

We must honour the past, but we do not have to live in the past!

8

The Big Question

Am I missing the burning bush for trying to keep the lawn cut?
Anon

So is this it? Revival, I mean!

A sign is there to make you wonder. One thing we can be sure of: where there are signs and wonders, there will be 'criticism following'! We have already noticed how, whenever Jesus healed the sick, performed a miracle or challenged the status quo, the Pharisees appeared out of nowhere! Carry on your priestly duties, ineffective though you may be, with major numerical haemorrhaging decade after decade, and you will barely raise a glimmer of interest. But fill your buildings, get some people laughing, crying, repenting and reconciled and have a few bodies on the floor, and out come the Pharisees!

The trouble is, in the West there is virtually nobody left alive who has experienced revival year after year. In this century the Welsh revival saw tens of thousands swept into the kingdom of God. It was underway by the end of 1904 and by the end of 1908 the fire was but a glimmer. There were many blessed memories and incredible stories, but they were nostalgic rather than prophetic.

There were a number of other isolated but brief revivals. Probably the most outstanding was on the Isle of Lewis in the Hebrides in the late 1940s and early 1950s. But they are few and far between.

Today laughter is sweeping many parts of the Western world in meetings of Christian people, but there is another factor in all revivals.

The fear factor

Thousands had been converted in Jerusalem, and many had returned home with the good news of Jesus Christ. Remarkable healings had taken place. A spirit of generosity (dare I say hilarity?) marked the early church. 'There were no needy persons among them. For from time to time, those who owned lands or houses sold them, brought the money from the sales and put it at the apostles' feet' (Acts 4:34–35).

But into that giving, generous, hilarious revival situation a couple of people sold some property and pretended they got less for it than they really did. It was the Apostle Peter (not simply judgement from heaven) who pronounced the death penalty on them both. I often hear people saying, 'I would love to go back to the New Testament church.' Personally, knowing my own heart, I would not. Having looked at the future (in the previous chapter), the future of Ananias and his wife Sapphira was to be short lived. And the result? 'Great fear seized the whole church and all who heard about these events' (Acts 5:11).

When angels made themselves known, it was not uncommon for their first words to be, 'Fear not.' When Jesus made himself known to his disciples after the crucifixion, his first words were, 'Fear not.' After abusing the grace of God there was 'great fear' upon the church. Why? Because they were afraid! Holy joy is only holy when it is matched by holy living. I don't mean static perfection, for as I have written elsewhere once we are born again sin is not an inevitability, it is only a possibility. But knowing it is a possibility, God has made full provision, allowing us to turn (repent), confess, receive forgiveness and the kiss of God's presence.

Holiness has to do with humility, being conscious of serving God, ensuring that his will and not ours is pursued. It also means confessing our sins, as well as our faults, to God and to one another as the Scriptures teach. It is because we are set apart from God that we are concerned with fulfilling the ordinary duties of life, going the extra 'mile' in service and relationships and, importantly, owning up when we get things wrong.

That is where Ananias and Sapphira went wrong. This was not a moment of unintentional insensitivity or foolishness. It was planned. Whenever God moves by his Spirit, whatever the fun-filled manifestations, there is a soberness which accompanies much of the rest of our activity.

David Brainerd saw a remarkable revival among the Indians of North America in the eighteenth century. In a journal he wrote:

Just at night the Lord visited me marvellously in prayer: I think my soul never was in such an agony before. I felt no restraint; the treasures of divine grace were open to me. I wrestled for absent friends, for the ingathering of souls, the children of God in many distant places. I was in such an agony, from some half an hour high, till near dark that I was all over wet with sweat. But yet it seemed to me that I had wasted away the day and had done nothing. Oh, my dear Jesus did sweat blood for souls! I long for more compassion towards them.

Fear and compassion seem to be hallmarks of true revival.

Revival journals

I currently live in Esher, Surrey, about eighteen miles from Westminster in London. My home town where I lived for forty years is a mere five minutes away by car. The last revival in my town was around 1860. Samuel Wesley Bradnack wrote in the *Methodist Recorder* of a meeting in a barn which still stands today.

> And now come with me to the Dining Hall. There was not a vacant seat in the chapel, there was not standing room in the Dining Hall. It is now 9 o'clock. The adult congregation is dismissed, but we cannot get rid of the children, they are crying for mercy. The foremost one is a youth of 16, a fearful drunkard he has been. He and 12 others as far as can be ascertained, last evening found peace with God.

In what was the greatest evangelical awakening since the days of Wesley and Whitefield, the revival crossed the Atlantic to Ulster in 1859. Among the converts were Dr Tom Barnardo, James Chalmers, Hugh Price-Hughes and Evan Hopkins of the Keswick Convention. Out of this group grew the Children's Special Service Mission (now the Scripture Union), the Salvation Army and the China Inland Mission. In seven years British Methodists grew by 200,000!

Wesley and Whitefield were no strangers to the manifestations of the Holy Spirit. On the first day of January 1739 in Fetter Lane Chapel at around 3 pm the Wesleys, Whitefield and four others explained:

The power of God came mightily upon us in so much that many cried out for exceeding joy, and many fell to the ground. As soon as we were recovered a little from awe and amazement at the presence of His Majesty, we broke out with one voice "we praise thee O God, we acknowledge thee to be the Lord . . ."

At a similar time in Northampton Jonathan Edwards wrote:

It is a very frequent thing to see outcries, faintings, convulsions and such like both with distress and also admiration and joy. It was not the manner here to hold meetings all night, nor was it common to continue them till very late in the night; but it was pretty often so that there were some so affected, and their bodies so overcome that they could not go home but were obliged to stay all night. (Jonathan Edwards, *An Account of the Revival of Religion in Northampton 1740–42*).

The brilliant evangelist C.H. Spurgeon declared, 'Revival is a season of glorious disorder.'

In *The Distinguishing Marks of a Work of the Spirit of God in 1741* Jonathan Edwards noted 'five sure, distinguishing Scripture evidences of revival':

1. It raises the esteem of Jesus in the community.
2. It works against the kingdom of Satan.
3. It stimulates a greater regard for the holy Scriptures.
4. It is marked by the Spirit of truth.
5. It is manifested by a renewed love of God and of man.

Of course every revival has had its critics, most of whom are church people who do not understand this sort of God. Dr Martyn Lloyd-Jones wrote:

Why should the devil suddenly start doing this kind of

thing? Here is the church in a period of dryness and drought, why should the devil suddenly do something which calls attention to religion and Jesus Christ? The very results of revival I would have thought, completely exclude the possibility of this being the action of the devil. If this is the work of the devil, well then, the devil is an unutterable fool. He is dividing his own kingdom; he is increasing the kingdom of God. There is nothing so ridiculous as this suggestion that this is the work of the devil.

He wrote elsewhere:

It comes near to being the rule that in revival phenomena begin to manifest themselves . . . sometimes people feel the power of the Spirit to such an extent that they faint and fall to the ground. Sometimes there are even convulsions, physical convulsions. And sometimes people seem to fall into a state of unconsciousness, into a kind of trance and many remain like that for hours . . . these phenomena are not essential to revival . . . yet it is true to say that, on the whole, they do tend to be present when there is a revival.

It was Wesley who noted: 'If we find a revival that is not spoken against we had better look again to ensure that it is a revival. No-one would pretend to claim that every revival burns with a smokeless flame.'

It was John Wesley who prayed: 'Lord, send us revival without its defects, but if this is not possible, send revival defects and all.' Careful people will assess the fruit of manifestations. Wise people will rejoice in what can be rejoiced in, but will be slow to put all phenomena down to God. It seems we are going to have to live in the tension of rejoicing, with caution!

A revival of the Spirit

Our bodies have not been born again! Our affections and emotions can therefore be motivated by the Holy Spirit, another spirit or carnal, fleshly motivation.

It was said that one of the greatest outpourings of the Holy Spirit in America was hindered through competitiveness. There were many churches and centres of spiritual activity, manifestations of Christ and unusual phenomena. Numbers grew, the gospel was preached and many were saved. But it was not long before competitiveness caused people to compare centre to centre, church to church, manifestation to manifestation. There were charges and counter-charges that the work here or there was deeper, richer, more meaningful, holier, more dynamic. The Holy Spirit was grieved and withdrew.

Perhaps that is why, amid the good and the bad, the Spirit and the flesh, the work of God and the work of the devil, we return to Scripture:

A new command I give you: Love one another. As I have loved you, so you must love one another (Jn 13:34).

Accept one another, then, just as Christ accepted you, in order to bring praise to God (Rom 15:7).

Be kind and compassionate to one another, forgiving each other, just as in Christ God forgave you (Eph 4:32).

And I pray that you, being rooted and established in love, may have power . . . to grasp how wide and long and high and deep is the love of Christ, and to know this love that surpasses knowledge—that you may be filled to the measure of all the fulness of God (Eph 3:17–19).

This well-known verse is preceded by Paul praying for the Ephesian church that God would 'strengthen you with power through his Holy Spirit'. But this is not power to do—it is power to be. It is power to be rooted and established in love, affecting all of our relationships, with our friends and our enemies, dealing competitiveness a death blow. We are merely servants. Even those in responsible positions must never forget that they are not leaders who serve, they are servants who lead.

As God leads us into the future there will be surprises; there will be the expected ordinariness that comes with familiar landmarks, responsibilities and commitments. But should we be privileged, as I believe we could be, to live through a time of sustained revival, we must put this 'moment' into perspective. It will shape our eternal destiny.

For further information about Pioneer's training courses, its evangelistic TIE Teams (Training In Evangelism) and its quarterly journal write to:

Pioneer
PO Box 79c
Esher
Surrey
KT10 9LP